P r a i s e   f o r

# A L E X   J .   H E R M O S I L L O

"His methods are unbelievably simple and fast. Energy Medicine appears to be one way for many to potentially help themselves and others quickly, effectively, and inexpensively. Attend one of his energy training sessions, and see for yourself."

—Doris J. Rapp, M.D.
Author of *Our Toxic World: A Wake Up Call*
and New York Times bestseller *Is This Your Child?*

"With ease and grace, you access spiritual power in a way that everyone…yes, anyone can easily apply and experience immediate results for themselves and others."

—Reverend Kyra Baehr
Unity of Divine Love Spiritual Center, Chandler, AZ

"Mesa IANDS is an association dedicated to the research, support, and education for people who have had, or are interested in the NDE (near death experience) and/or the OBE (out of body experience). Alex J. Hermosillo spoke to the Mesa IANDS chapter, and he was a hit. Alex shared the wisdom he gained from heaven during his NDE. Yet, it was his honest transparency and completely loving attitude that won the audience over. When you meet Alex you are impressed with his loving, helpful, and kind nature. His focus is on you, and one cannot help but like him immediately. Alex brings healing and peace to people who are grieving due to the death of a loved one. As a speaker on near death experiences or the power of his healing, I would recommend Alex Hermosillo for any group, at any time."

—Larry Merril
Coordinator of the Mesa chapter of the International Association
for Near Death Studies, www.iands.org

A TRUE STORY OF

# HOPE, HEALING AND MIRACLES

First published in 2011 by
RainbowLight Creations, LLC
with offices at:
1415 E. Guadalupe Road., Suite 106
Tempe, AZ 85283 U.S.A.

www.rainbowlightcreations.com

Cover artwork and text design by Bill Greaves, Concept West.
Interior layout by 1106 Design
Illustrations by Michelle Kondrich and Paige Sullivan

ISBN: 978-0-9838565-0-4

A TRUE STORY OF

# HOPE, HEALING AND MIRACLES

## ALEX J. HERMOSILLO

RAINBOWLIGHT
CREATIONS

# AUTHOR'S NOTE

This is a true story.

Some of the names of individuals mentioned in this book
have been changed to protect their privacy.

I dedicate this book in loving memory of my father,
Romeo Hermosillo, and my mother, Mercedes Hermosillo.

This book is also dedicated to Amy LaLicata, the Light in my life,
and to those of you who are searching for Light, Love, and Healing.

# ACKNOWLEDGMENTS

I would like to thank my father, Romeo Hermosillo, for teaching me courage and strength, and my mother, Mercedes Hermosillo, for sharing with me her joy, love, and compassion. Thank you both for bringing me into this beautiful world.

I deeply and lovingly thank Amy LaLicata for always believing in me, and for encouraging me to follow my true course of destiny to do God's work. Taking several years off from her career in the movie industry, she helped me write this book about my life and managed my healing center. Thank you very much, Amy. You are truly an earth angel, and I am blessed that you are my Love.

There are simply no words that can express the gratitude and love I have for Maria for saving my life, for loving me, and for caring about me through the most difficult and challenging times in my life.

I would also like to thank all of my clients, students, and friends. As our paths crossed, we gained wisdom together, and together our Light shines brighter for humanity. Special mention goes to Father Jorge Eagar, Julie George, Glen Phillips, Bill Schreiner, Randy Benowitz, Char Mada, Soleil Dolce, and my brother Eddie for your friendships and permission to share your stories with the readers. To the others whom I cannot mention by name because of unwanted attention, thank you for allowing us to include your stories of healing in this book. To Sheila and Reverend Jenn: Thank you for your gracious help and support.

To all the loving individuals who helped in editing this book: Susan Torres, Amelia Sheldon, and especially Diane LaLicata for her countless hours of work and enduring enthusiasm. To Jodi Brandon, who took this book and nurtured it with vigilant care for the final edit before it was published, thank you. And to four earth angels, Candi and Joe Roach and Diane and Charles LaLicata, who through their loving support and generosity, helped to make this book possible.

To all the heavenly beings, angels, and the one we call God: Thank you for always being with me. Thank you for your guidance. Thank you for your unconditional love.

# CONTENTS

*"To touch the lives of others,
to assist them so they can
experience a happy, healthy, and
loving life; there is no greater joy."*

~ Alex J. Hermosillo

# AN OPENING WORD

In the summer of 1996, while visiting a small Mexican border town for business, the gift of healing was awakened within me as a woman handed her six-month-old dying baby girl to me and she spontaneously healed. Soon after, I had a near-death experience in a hospital emergency room, where a second gift was given to me. I learned there is no such thing as death—only a new beginning.

Along my journey, I have been blessed to assist people in healing their migraine headaches, backaches, cancer, heart disease, tumors, depression, and more. During their healing sessions and in my classes, many of them and I have seen, heard, and/or felt the presence of angels and other heavenly beings, bringing the awareness to us all that we are never alone.

Many call me a healer. I think of myself as a man like any other who has chosen to be in service to others—to share with you the gifts that were given to me—the gifts of Light, Love, and Healing.

This is my story.

*Alex J. Hermosillo*

# CHAPTER ONE

# THE GIFT AWAKENS

## Summer 1996

I always enjoyed making the five-hour drive through southern Arizona to San Luis, Mexico. The drive away from the hustle and bustle of the big city of Phoenix through the Sonoran Desert is tranquil and beautiful, with its many large Saguaro cactuses standing like sentinels at attention. Some of these giants have been in position for hundreds of years. They would feel like my protectors as I drove south, ushering me toward a place of comfort. This small, festive border town is welcoming, with its aroma of food cooking along a main street dotted with brightly colored tourist shops. On one particular trip, the town's relaxed atmosphere was soothing to me after a long, hectic workweek in sales. Any stress I had was left behind when I crossed the U.S. border into Mexico.

*Friday night, at last!* My excitement built while I parked my car in the dusty parking lot of the small, cozy restaurant that my brother Eddie and I owned in San Luis. Painted in Old World Spanish turquoise on the outside, the old building that seemed small surprisingly could accommodate up to fifty people for dining. In contrast to its exterior Spanish, the restaurant's interior had a modern style with a large-screen TV, sleek stainless steel barstools, and tables covered in bright blue leather. A tiny two-bedroom home sat a short distance behind the restaurant; we used it as a guesthouse. Stepping out of my car into the warm summer night, I had no idea that an event later that evening would change my life and the lives of those closest to me forever.

Nearing the restaurant, I could hear one of the latest American Top 40 songs resound loudly from our state-of-the-art stereo system. The place was half full of U.S. Marines from the Marine base in Yuma, Arizona, just twenty miles away. They were comfortable visiting our restaurant, knowing that Eddie and I are Americans and that we served in the U.S. military. (As a young man, I enlisted in the Navy, and Eddie served in the Army.) In a futile attempt to make being away from their families a little more bearable, the Marines were gearing up for a night on the town visiting local nightclubs and bars.

My brother Eddie was working hard in the small kitchen. "What's up, Chico?" he asked, glad to see me. (*Chico* means "little boy" in Spanish and is a nickname that was given to me by one of my sisters on the day I was born, weighing in at only five and a half pounds.) After we greeted each other, Eddie and I joined our friends who lived in San Luis. While we chatted with them, more customers arrived, ordered their food, and joined friends. After sharing conversation with our group, I excused myself and walked outside for some fresh air. Eddie followed me. Standing just outside the restaurant's doorway, we looked down the street now crowded with partygoers laughing and calling out to each other.

When I was a small boy of nine and Eddie only four, our family lived for about a year in San Luis. My father first saw my mother in this town many years before, when he accompanied his father on a business trip. His father brought a movie camera along on the trip to film family and friends. While my father was filming he unknowingly captured the image of a pretty, young girl who would later become my mother. A short time later, my father purchased land here, and he built a house and two apartment complexes. As a result, my parents, my nine siblings, and I visited San Luis often through the years.

Soon an employee stepped outside to inquire about additional food supplies; it was close to eleven o'clock at night, and the restaurant continued to fill with hungry customers waiting to be served. Eddie returned to the kitchen, and I helped serve the food that he quickly prepared. Hours passed, as did the beers, and by two o'clock in the morning I was exhausted. Eddie continued to cook some last-minute orders, so on my way through the kitchen I told him that I was leaving for the little house to count the day's sales receipts.

Walking through the old, small house, I was reminded that there was not much to look at: a tiny kitchen, an empty living room, a single bathroom, and two small bedrooms, with only a mattress in each. While sitting on one of the mattresses counting receipts, I thought I heard someone calling my name. I got up and quickly walked toward the sound, coming from the direction of the living room, and I caught a glimpse of my friend Dulce and my brother Eddie rushing toward the house.

Dulce and her husband were good friends of ours. They had assisted Eddie and me with the preparation for our restaurant's grand opening six months before. Dulce was 23 years old, and for as long as I have known her, she has been a very positive and happy person. But that night Dulce's beautiful, long black hair was hanging across her face like a spider web, wet from tears. Clutching her six-month-old baby, she cried out, "Alex, my baby is ill. She has a 103 temperature and can hardly breathe! Please help me! Don't let her die!" The closest hospital to San Luis was fifteen miles away, and I guessed that Dulce feared her baby wouldn't survive the long trip.

Without hesitation I told her I would try to help them. Dulce quickly placed the sick baby in my arms. I was shocked when I heard myself tell Dulce that she should wait in the restaurant for just a few minutes and that I would call for her. Looking at me with hope and desperation on her face, Dulce resolutely turned to leave. While holding Dulce's baby in my arms, I watched her and Eddie make their way across the parking lot toward the restaurant. I was then standing alone in the doorway with Dulce's baby.

Returning to the bedroom, I quickly glanced down at the baby's limbs hanging limply. They appeared lifeless. Laying the baby gently on top of the mattress, I took a curious and closer look at her tiny body. Her nasal passages were closed over, making it difficult for her to breathe, and her skin was a reddish color with what appeared to be a rash over her body. Her eyes were closed, and she was gasping for air. Judging from the sound of her breathing, I believed her lungs were congested.

A strong urge suddenly enveloped me, and for unknown reasons, I placed my hands four inches above her tiny body, closed my eyes, and forcefully cried out, *"You are healed!"* A strange rush of energy filled my body, expanded outward, and eventually engulfed the entire room. Time slowed for me and then stopped, making it seem like there was no beginning or end to the present moment. Another burst of energy surged through me, this time flowing through my arms and out of my hands. My body tingled from head to toe, and I could feel my hands heat up like they were on fire. Then the tingling sensation faded, my hands cooled down, and everything felt peaceful. The room was quiet. I was astonished at what I saw when I slowly opened my eyes. The baby's eyes were open and sparkling with new life. Her breathing seemed normal to me. Her nasal passages were no longer clogged, and the redness of her skin had disappeared. I glanced at the small wind-up clock sitting on the nightstand, and I noticed only a few minutes had passed. Turning my attention back to the baby, I touched her forehead and it felt cooler, the fever gone. Unable to believe or comprehend what I was seeing, I only could guess that a miracle must have occurred! An overwhelming feeling of fear within me followed that thought.

I fell to my knees with my head bowed and hands placed over my face. My heart was pounding uncontrollably. Raising my head toward heaven, I cried out, *"Oh, my God! Oh, my God! Oh, my God!"* Without thinking, my hands moved across my heart in an attempt to comfort it, while tears streamed down my cheeks. I could not deny the divine presence or power in that tiny bedroom; intuitively I knew that the only choice was to surrender to this experience. I humbly lowered my head again and focused my attention on the small baby girl who was then alertly looking up at me. Her sparkling eyes were glowing, and she began to speak out in baby language. I was happy with the thought that she was telling me she was okay.

I took several deep breaths, wiped the tears from my face, and attempted to compose myself. Carefully lifting the baby off the mattress and holding her close to my chest, I walked out of the house and headed toward the restaurant's rear entrance. After opening the door and taking a few steps inside, I called out, "Dulce!" She rushed toward me and I happily handed her the child, saying that her baby would be okay. The look of fear and despair that had been etched on Dulce's face was quickly replaced with a look of pure joy. After hugging and thanking me over and over, she quickly sat at a vacant table to admire her healthy child. What a wonderful moment in time, watching Dulce smiling, talking to, and playing with her baby. She looked up for a moment and thanked me once again. Not knowing what to say or how to explain to Dulce what had happened in the tiny house, I just acknowledged her with a slight nod.

I felt odd, like I was in a vacuum; the silence that seemed to surround me was deafening. I had the perception of being suspended in time. I heard a faint voice calling out to me. Slowly the voice strengthened and pulled me back to the present moment. The mysterious voice was Eddie's. I realized, after gathering my thoughts, that Eddie needed my help in the kitchen. I quickly found myself back in the swing of things: getting the next day's supplies ready and serving last-minute customers before the restaurant closed.

In bed that night thinking about the baby's healing, I tried to soothe myself by wrapping my arms around my chest. Exhausted from the day's events, I quickly fell asleep.

Looking in the bathroom mirror while shaving the next morning, I again began to wonder what happened the previous night. Was the entire incident with Dulce's baby a dream, or did it really happen? Why did she come to me? Why did I tell Dulce I would call her in a couple of minutes? How did I know I would only be a couple of minutes? Why did I place my hands over her sick child? Where did that awareness and information come from? Why did I say, *"You are healed!"*? I stared at my hands, but they appeared normal to me. Physically, when I looked at my hands, face, and body, nothing had changed. However, in some way I thought I looked different when I looked into the bathroom mirror for a second time, though I was unable to pinpoint any physical change.

Fastening my watch, I realized that it was time to leave for the restaurant. Eddie and our manager, Juan, were sitting in the small kitchen drinking cups of coffee. I grabbed a large cup and joined them. They immediately asked me about Dulce's baby, because they knew how quickly the child was returned to its mother. Almost apologetically I said, "I just placed my hands on the baby and she was healed. I don't understand why or how." Juan had heard stories through the years about places in Mexico where healers are able to heal with their hands. In an attempt to change to another topic I adamantly told Juan, "I am not one of those people!" Eddie was insistent about wanting to know how I was able to help Dulce's baby; I answered him the same way: "I don't know. I just don't know." Eddie finally relented, but Juan wanted to look at my hands to see if he could feel anything come out of them. Standing up to pour myself another cup of coffee, I told them both, "Give me a break! It was beautiful and amazing but also frightening to me, and I don't want to talk about it anymore!" Then, looking at my watch, I reminded them that it was time to start preparing for the luncheon customers, who would be arriving soon. Thankfully, we quickly switched to discussing the day's responsibilities.

The story of the baby's healing was retold a few times during the following week. Eddie told our mother and a close friend of the family, and then it was not mentioned again. The memory of that unimaginable event faded away and my life returned to normal, or so it seemed.

# CHAPTER TWO

# MY JOURNEY
# TO HEAVEN

## Fall 1997

"Alex," my mother's voice called out from the other side of my bedroom door. "Get up. It's eight o'clock!"

October 10, 1997 was another workday. As I glanced around the bedroom, a feeling of contentment and comfort filled me. I looked outside my window and saw that the weather was beautiful at my parents' home in Mesa, Arizona. When my short-lived marriage ended, my parents lovingly opened their home to me, gladly providing me with parental nurturing and whatever time I needed to heal. Both my wife and I felt we were not a good match together, so we agreed to part ways. My brother Eddie was also living in my parents' home while attending college at Arizona State University. We took turns running errands, and we happily helped our parents in any way we could. Added bonuses for me were Mom's home cooking and a very short drive to work.

That morning unfolded like most. After showering and dressing, I ate a small breakfast with my mother, a wonderful, giving woman whom I dearly love. Her tiny nose held a pair of small, round-shaped glasses for her near-sightedness, and we talked about my brothers and sisters, her aches and pains, and upcoming doctor appointments for both her and my father while we ate.

Time quickly passed and too soon it was time to leave for work. Kissing my mother's head, I told her that I loved her. As I headed down the hallway toward Dad's bedroom, I remembered to tell Mom that I'd see her for lunch. Slowly opening Dad's bedroom door, I saw him pulling a shirt over his thin frame. He was once a strong and robust man, but aging had left him small in stature. After we chatted briefly, he wished me a good day at work.

After work, I joined my brothers and one of my sisters at our favorite pool hall. For such a large family, we had remained quite close, and we thoroughly enjoyed each other's company whenever we could get together. Eddie and I played a few games of pool, and we enjoyed several dances with our sister and several of her girlfriends. Later that evening, Eddie suggested that I ask a girl, standing alone near the dance floor, to dance. Hesitating for a moment because I was enjoying the time with my family and friends, I eventually relented and agreed to meet her.

Approaching the pretty stranger, I noticed that she was Hispanic, with long black hair and beautiful brown eyes. I asked her to dance as heavy metal music played in the background.

With a serious face she asked, "To this song? I don't think so!"

"What about a different song?" I asked.

"Well, maybe," she answered.

Reaching my hand out toward her, I introduced myself: "Hi. My name is Alex."

Shaking my hand, she said her name was Maria. It was impossible to talk while the music boomed loudly in the background, so I suggested that we continue our conversation on the patio, hoping it would be quieter outside.

Maria was quick to tell me that she was a single mother with three children. I suspected she was wondering if that information would send me running for my life. I told Maria that I love children, that I'm one of ten, and that I have plenty of nieces and nephews. I added that four of my siblings lived in California and the six youngest children, including me, lived in the Phoenix area. Maria was originally from Fresno, California, and had one brother and one sister who still lived there. She moved with her three children to Mesa, Arizona, a city within the Phoenix metropolitan area, and was working as a nurse. I shared that I worked in sales and that I was living temporarily with my parents and my brother Eddie.

After talking for several hours with Maria about our lives and dreams, I felt as if I had always known her. We exchanged phone numbers before we left the pool hall. Thinking about how nice Maria was while driving home, I decided to call her the next day, with the hope of seeing her again. The following morning I was surprised by a phone call from Maria asking if I would like to have dinner with her that evening. I agreed, flattered and delighted that she had called. We thoroughly enjoyed each other's company during dinner, and we agreed to see each other the next evening as well.

There was a steady flow of customers at work, where I sold major home appliances, the following day. Outside, hot dogs were being grilled for employees. After quickly grabbing a chili dog during my lunch break, I headed home to relax a bit before my afternoon shift began. After I returned to work, heartburn symptoms suddenly flared up, and they quickly turned into an upset stomach. Thinking that I might have the stomach flu, I decided to return home again.

Feeling even worse at home, I headed straight to bed. After pulling the covers over me, I suddenly remembered that Maria and I had plans to go out after work. I made a quick call to cancel our date. Still wanting to see me, Maria suggested picking me up to watch movies at her apartment. Reassuringly, she said, "Alex, remember: I'm a nurse, and I can take care of you." Happily, I agreed to her plan. Certainly, having her take care of me had to be better than suffering alone! I reassured my parents that I would be fine in Maria's company. Besides, this was an opportunity for my parents to meet Maria.

When Maria arrived, she had a brief conversation with my parents and then we began the half-hour drive to her apartment. As we were driving, my discomfort increased dramatically. Soon I was feeling dizzy while having chills and intense hot flashes. I felt as though I was going to be sick. I told Maria, and she quickly exited the freeway and pulled into the parking lot of a fast food restaurant.

Bolting from her car, I raced into the restaurant and headed straight for the men's restroom. The dizzy spell suddenly worsened and my legs became weak, causing me to collapse before reaching the restroom door. I passed out briefly, and when I came to I was lying on the floor looking straight at the door. I crawled into the small bathroom and locked the door behind me. I became violently sick to my stomach. After losing consciousness a second time, I opened my eyes to find myself lying on the bathroom floor in a small pool of brownish-red liquid! I couldn't have been lying on the floor too long, I guessed, or someone would have found me. I was able to pull myself up off the bathroom floor by grabbing the edge of the bathroom sink. I was feeling extremely ill. While splashing water on my face it occurred to me that I better get out of the bathroom and get some help. As hard as it was to believe, I thought that if I failed to do this I would die right there.

I returned unsteadily to Maria, who was patiently waiting in her car, and mumbled to her that I collapsed in the bathroom. She quickly drove the two blocks to her apartment. I was still feeling weak and light-headed, so Maria helped me into her bed. Again though, I felt nauseous and went right back into the bathroom with her. Wide-eyed, Maria anxiously said, "Alex, it's all blood! I need to get you to the hospital!"

At the hospital, a flurry of emergency room doctors and nurses moved quickly around me. I could feel myself going in and out of consciousness. When I was awake the action around me seemed to move in slow motion. Then I experienced a sudden silence! I had a peaceful feeling within me, and I sensed myself rising toward the sky. Slowly and gently I rose until I was floating above what appeared to be a golden mist, and I could no longer see the nurses, doctors, or medical equipment. Curiously, though, I could see Maria, my mother, my father, and all nine of my siblings. All of my loved ones were standing in a straight row, surrounded by the golden mist. They were looking up at me with amazed expressions on their faces. We just stared at each other. I had a feeling that my time on Earth was over, so I smiled at them and waved goodbye. I felt no attachment to them, nor did I have any concern about leaving them behind.

Excitement built within me as I looked up and accelerated toward the clouds. I extended my arms out in front of me and flew like Superman because I felt a necessity to quickly reach some unknown destination. Then a thought came to me: If I pulled my arms straight down along my sides I could lessen the wind resistance, which I did, enabling me to fly faster and faster!

As I broke through the clouds at a tremendous speed, layers upon layers of grief, fear, heartache, and pain from my life were being pulled from the top of my head, down through my body, and out of the bottoms of my feet. I felt lighter and lighter. Soon, I held nothing but joy. Unfathomable and immeasurable *joy* surrounded and filled me completely. There simply are no earthly words to accurately describe this experience.

A bright pinpoint of light suddenly appeared ahead, and I became extremely excited! *"Faster! Faster! Faster!"* I cried out, wanting to get to the bright light as soon as possible. As I entered the Light I became one with it; there was no beginning and no end. Somehow I had a knowledge that the Light always was and always will be. I was in bliss! With an awareness of love so great and profound, I knew I was home in the presence of God!

I looked around at that magnificent place of peace and love, and I could see what appeared to be beings emanating light. They were everywhere—all around me, hundreds of them. Focusing more closely, I had the impression they were souls who had lived on Earth. Strangely, the light from some of these souls was bright and strong, while others' light appeared dim and weak. With a simple inquiry of this phenomenon, a knowingness came to me that the strength of their light reflected who they were, as individuals, during their time on Earth. If an individual was loving, kind, and helpful to others, his or her soul's light was very bright. If they were judgmental, angry, and selfish, their light was dim. At that moment, I understood that all suffering, pain, and disease was due to the lack of light.

I understood that the light of these souls, in its purest form, was a loving, creative, and nurturing energy that grows brighter and stronger depending on the love the souls had for themselves and others. I couldn't help noticing a few souls whose light was shining so brightly that it was like looking at the sun. These souls, I believe, were like the great teachers on Earth such as Jesus, Buddha, Krishna, Mother Mary, Ghandi, Mother Teresa, and Martin Luthar King.

One of the brightest beings of Light approached me. I could *feel* its magnificent presence and wisdom, and I began to absorb information from it. What I can only describe as a blessing or an awakening was occurring within me. I understood that the Light holds information about who we are, why we come to Earth, and where we are going. On Earth and in Heaven, it is important that we shine our Light as bright as possible, not only for ourselves, but for our loved ones and for all life.

Life does not end on Earth. Our souls continue their journey in the place we call Heaven. The greater an individual's love and peace, the greater his or her wisdom, and the brighter his or her soul's Light shines. But ultimately, we are all made of this loving, creative, and nurturing Light—the Light we call God.

While I was enjoying this wondrous experience, I began to hear distant beeping sounds and my blissful journey abruptly ended. I opened my eyes to look around. I saw that I was back in a hospital bed with the sound of a medical monitor beeping by my side. Realizing I was no longer in that magnificent place of love and peace, I tightly closed my eyes and wished myself back there. I waited, but nothing happened. A profound sadness came over me, and I soon gave up trying to get back to the place of complete joy, freedom, light, and love. My sadness quickly turned to anger, and cursing, I questioned why I had to return to a hospital bed, hooked up to monitors and intravenous tubes.

"Alex, are you okay?" A voice caught my attention.

Focusing my eyes, I saw Maria standing at the foot of the bed. Oddly, she looked different to me. I was amazed that I was able to *feel* and see her Light, a beautiful energy that was emanating from her physical body. This was something I had never experienced before. "I'm okay," I told her half-heartedly.

Maria walked to the side of the bed and kissed me softly on my forehead, replacing my anger with a warm feeling that somehow made it okay to be back. Maria said she had gone to my home to inform my family what had happened. She and Eddie returned to the hospital emergency room and stayed with me throughout the evening as I went in and out of consciousness. She said the doctors couldn't find any cause for the bleeding.

Maria and I continued to grow closer. She visited me daily during my four-day stay at the hospital and the following few weeks at home during my recuperation. I didn't tell her or any family members about my incredible "into the Light" experience. I would have had a hard time describing it to anyone. The only thing I was sure about was that Maria saved my life. With her one kiss in the hospital that day, my thoughts and feelings shifted from not wanting to return to this life to a feeling of gratitude toward the one who helped me remain alive. I was okay about being here, with Maria, to continue my journey on earth.

# CHAPTER THREE

# AN OUT-OF-BODY EXPERIENCE

## Fall 1997

Two weeks after my release from the hospital, I continued to recuperate in the loving care of my family. I had seen the doctor several times since leaving the hospital, but he was unable to find a reason for what happened to me. Tests were run but, unfortunately, they were inconclusive. The doctor's final diagnosis was a ruptured blood vessel in my intestinal tract due to vomiting. Other than attending my scheduled doctor's appointments, I had not ventured outside my parents' home.

Still slightly weak and somewhat unsteady on my feet, one day I took a refreshingly long, hot shower in preparation for a visit to see my co-workers. As I left the house and walked toward my parked car, I was struck by the wonderful day. The sky, trees, birds, and all of nature looked so brilliant to me. I saw colors and I heard sounds I had never even noticed before. Sliding into the front seat, part of me recognized how content I was and how absolutely beautiful life is.

I was fortunate as a salesperson to have achieved the success I had working for a large retail chain. As soon as I entered the store's appliance section I noticed co-workers going about their usual duties. I was surprised by my extreme awareness of the surroundings and by a feeling I can only describe as heaviness around me. While I chatted with co-workers inquiring about my health, I noticed that there was a slight glow around their bodies. I was also surprised by the fact that my body felt differently during individual conversations. I came to realize that I was physically responding in an exaggerated and specific way to each person. While one person felt light and gentle to me, another felt heavy and dense. I began to get a headache and my stomach started to churn. I didn't understand what was happening to me. I became so uncomfortable that I quickly said my goodbyes and left for home.

After returning home I felt much better, but I wondered what on earth had happened in the store. I never before experienced anything like the shifting sensations I had when I spoke to different people. I felt unsettled. I was certain about one thing: Feeling the way I did around my co-workers was anything but pleasurable! I felt detached from them, and I couldn't help but wonder what was wrong with me and whether this feeling would last.

I learned a long while later that I had become what is termed "empathic." Because of my near-death and out-of-body purification experience, emptied of my own negative emotions, painful memories, and physical ailments, I began to feel, physically and emotionally, what other people felt. I could feel their peace and joy, but I also knew their grief and pain. I felt them within my body and felt their emotions as if they were my own. In other words, in the company of loving people, I felt good. Many times, though, when I was in the company of physically ailing, negative attitudes, or emotionally hurt people, I felt ill. I became a pure vessel, so to speak, which made me extremely sensitive to everything and everyone!

As the days passed, I was spending most of my time recuperating at home. (Thankfully, I had weeks of sick pay in reserve, so I had no concerns for lost income, and I was able to focus on my health.) Maria called one morning and said she wanted to see me. I felt comfortable, and my body was non-agitated around my parents, Eddie, and Maria, so I told her that I was looking forward to seeing her. I couldn't help but wonder if Maria's visit would be a difficult one for her. The last time she had been in my parents' home was to tell them and Eddie that I was in the hospital. She told me it was a very emotional time for all of them.

After Maria arrived at the house, she chatted with Mom for a short time, and we both visited with Dad in his bedroom. Everyone was getting along perfectly, and I sensed that my parents really liked her, especially my dad. Because I was feeling really well being with her, I asked Maria to have lunch with me at a nearby restaurant. I was a little concerned about being in public again, and we sat in a small booth at the restaurant. There were many customers and quite of bit of activity around us, yet I was able to sustain balance within myself, both physically and emotionally, as long as I focused on Maria. We thoroughly enjoyed our lunch together, and it felt so good to be able to relax in public again. Maria and I had a wonderful afternoon, and we continued to see each other nearly every day.

My strength was slowly returning to normal, and I was again getting comfortable during family functions. I met Maria's children, Donna, Joey, and David, and together we began attending family festivities. During one family event, Maria and I shared our hearts and spoke the words "I love you" to each other.

After several more weeks of recuperation I returned to work, careful to keep some distance between certain co-workers and me. I felt wonderful having some normalcy in my life once again, and I sincerely hoped the normalcy was not short-lived. Before my first morning at work was over, the store manager asked me to meet him in his office. When he started speaking, I felt myself suddenly pulled from my body, and I was hovering at what appeared to be twenty feet in the air above the two of us. Mimicking my emergency room experience, I could feel negativity pulling out of me, leaving me with a sensation of pure peace. But, unlike the first time, I didn't go into the Light. Instead I was just looking down at my boss and my own physical body, observing our meeting while it unfolded. With no emotional attachment to my body, the store manager, or the event itself, I was simply observing. Suddenly I had a sensation, or realization, that I was not on Earth or in Heaven. I felt like I was a pure spirit, disconnected, and experiencing what seemed to me a middle realm of existence.

I felt my spirit slowly re-enter my body before the manager finished talking. The energies of my spirit and physical body reconnected, but unexpectedly an overwhelming sense of fear shot through me. My heart was pounding and I thought to myself, "*I need to get away from here.*" Leaving the manager's office and returning to the sales floor trembling and in a daze, I was certain I had lost all control of my own life and body! After standing around in a stupor on the sales floor for a few minutes, I told a co-worker I was feeling ill and needed to leave.

On the way to my parents' home, I stopped at the closest grocery store, and bought a six-pack of beer and a bottle of vodka. Returning home, I immediately headed for my room. Anger was building inside of me, and I was extremely upset with God. This was the second time I unwillingly left my body, and I was frustrated because I couldn't control this *thing*—whatever this *thing* was that was happening to me. Furthermore, how could I control *it* if I didn't understand what *it* was, or why *it* was? Why did this keep happening to me? What was wrong with me? I was really scared, plain and simple! I drank some of the alcohol I bought and cried myself to sleep.

Maria continued to be my best friend and confidante. We loved and enjoyed each other tremendously, but I couldn't help but feel I might frighten her if I shared the story of my out-of-body experience with her. I was so sure she would feel frightened because that was how I was feeling! So I kept all of the questioning, stress, worry, and sensations I had of being powerless in my own life to myself. I didn't tell my friends or my family. I was scared and I felt that no one would understand.

Feeling alone and full of despair, I had an increasingly difficult time going to work. Just knowing that the mere presence of some co-workers would make me ill, I became more and more anxious by the day. I continued to try my best to uphold my personal and financial responsibilities, and I continued to turn to alcohol for the escape I needed from these new, overwhelming developments in my life.

# CHAPTER FOUR

# MY MOTHER'S HEALING

## Fall 1997

A few weeks after my second out-of-body episode, my mother experienced severe stomach pains and visited her doctor. Tests revealed that she had gallbladder stones. During surgery, oxygen tubes were placed in her nose and down her throat. Because of this procedure, she experienced terrible nosebleeds when she returned home. We rushed her to the hospital, where doctors cauterized the veins in her nose on multiple occasions, but the procedure was unsuccessful, as her nosebleeds inevitably returned.

A few weeks later, on my day off of work, the only sound in the house while my parents napped was the TV. I was in the living room watching my favorite movie, *Operation Pacific*, starring John Wayne. (Dad was a Marine at Guadalcanal during World War II, and that always made this movie especially interesting to me.) While I was totally engrossed in the movie, as the Marines were landing on the beach of Guadalcanal and taking heavy casualties, Mom suddenly cried, "Alex! Help me!" Turning my head around toward the direction of her voice, I caught a glimpse of Mom running from her bedroom toward me with both hands cupped over her nose and mouth as she desperately tried to contain the blood pouring out of her nose. Because I was feeling somewhat put out, I thought, "*What a time for this to happen, just when the Marines are landing on the beach!*"

Just like it did when I was handed Dulce's baby in Mexico, a strong sense of what I call "knowingness" came over me. I instructed Mom to sit in the chair, and then I stood up next to her with my attention still glued to the television. Without consciously thinking about it, I extended my right arm out in front of her face with my hand positioned only inches away from her nose. I sensed time slow down again. What seemed like the passing of several hours was just a single minute or two. I felt a surge of energy run through my body, bursting out of my hand, and my body became hot. But for some reason, I was more distracted by the movie than I was with what was happening between my mother and me. Mom suddenly let out a cry so piercing and frightening it made me turn and make a mad dash to my bedroom without looking back! I quickly locked the door behind me.

I was frightened by her scream, and tears poured from my eyes. I cried, "Oh, my God! Oh, my God!" as I paced back and forth in my small bedroom. I frantically pleaded, "I've killed her! Oh, my God! I've killed my mother! Please, God! Don't let her be dead!" I truly believed I had killed my mother with the mysterious power in my hands. And, shamefully, the reason I killed her was that I was too focused on what was happening on television! Questions and dark thoughts were flashing through my mind: "How will I explain this to Father, who's napping in the bedroom, or to my brothers and sisters?" I was sure that only my dying would satisfy the guilt I felt at that point.

Gathering all the confidence I could, I decided I needed to check on Mom. Slowly I unlocked the bedroom door and, as I entered the living room, I saw her sitting quietly on the sofa like she was in a daze. She removed her hands from around her mouth and nose, looked up at me surprised, and exclaimed that the bleeding had stopped. "That's good, Mom," I answered her.

I was so overwhelmed by the entire event that, without saying goodbye to her, I walked straight out of the house, got into my car, and drove to a nearby bar. My mother's nose never bled again.

I suddenly realized that, in a relatively short period of time, I had one near-death experience, had an out-of-body journey, began to feel or sense other people's joy and pain, and just experienced another powerful energy flow surge through my body that resulted in a second spontaneous healing. All of this happened within sixty days! As amazing and intriguing as I thought this was at the time, underneath it all I felt cursed, not blessed. I didn't understand what was happening to me. I felt overwhelmed and out of control, and I was quickly becoming a nervous wreck!

# CHAPTER FIVE

# THE LOST YEARS: FEAR OF CHANGE

## Spring 1998

I prayed to God for answers after my mother's healing. No answers came. Five months had passed since her nosebleeds and six months since my hospital visit. I was no longer able to relate to co-workers or my job. I had doubts about who I was and where my life was heading, and I was paranoid about the possibility of being pulled out of my body without warning. I was afraid to touch anyone and feared that a surge of energy might explode out of my hands at any moment. It was a scary and unsettling time for me.

I desperately reached out to two of my brothers, sharing with them about the energy sporadically coming out from my hands and my feelings of confusion, but they didn't understand. I didn't blame them: How could they possibly understand when I didn't understand myself? They began to avoid any conversation with me about my troublesome life. They said I was "nuts" or told jokes about me. Taking the hint, I avoided talking with them about recent happenings.

Maria reacted somewhat differently. She was able to feel a tingling sensation and heat radiate from my hands, so she was certain that I had the ability to heal. Maria did her best to understand and comfort me, but, just like my brothers, she was frightened. Who could really fault her? I, too, was frightened!

There was a time when I considered myself a strong and confident man, but at that time I felt broken. Even with Maria's support my world was a place of turmoil; I didn't know where to turn or whom to turn to for help. As fate would have it, an acquaintance of mine introduced me to the world of drugs. I soon found my drug of choice, methamphetamine. It worked just fine.

Methamphetamine allowed me to escape the pain of my reality, and it provided a freedom from my fears. The drug soon consumed me and took over my life. I started calling in "sick" to work so I was able to get more sleep and buy more drugs. Just months earlier, my priorities were clear: family, Maria and her children, and career. I had become more interested in a drug to help me escape a life I used to love! Sometimes it occurred to me that I was becoming an addict. I had some money saved and was financially fine for the time being, but my money was dwindling, along with my self-esteem.

I wondered whether Maria was aware of my addiction, because she never confronted me about it. I guessed she wasn't sure how to go about it. Perhaps she was afraid our relationship might end or that my addiction wasn't real if she didn't think about it. Whatever her reason, I was very aware that my drug addiction was taking a toll on Maria and her children. I was ashamed about what I was doing to myself and to Maria and her family, but by that time the drug had a terrible hold on me.

One night, Maria was restless and having trouble sleeping. With a strong desire to comfort her overriding any concerns I had for potentially hurting her on that particular evening, I placed my right hand on the middle of her back and said silently while imagining the peace and love in the Light I experienced in Heaven, "I send you Light, Love, and Healing." Within minutes Maria was quietly asleep, and I slowly removed my hand from her back. I smiled to myself, feeling good that I was able to help Maria. Relaxing while looking at the ceiling, I felt myself abruptly, and without warning, pulled off the bed in an upward direction at such excessive speed that I can only describe it as one million miles per hour! Like a bullet fired from a gun, I shot upward and out through the roof of Maria's small apartment, heading straight into the night sky. The force of the speed was tremendous, creating a ripple feeling on my face and arms. I tried to yell out loud, but it was too difficult. It felt like the air in my lungs was being sucked out, and in that moment I was sure I was going to die!

My fear became overwhelming as I got closer and closer to the stars. Just as suddenly as it began, my speeding body stopped, and I was floating in space. A great sense of relief came over me while I glanced around at the expansive space in a state of peace. This space where I found myself was unimaginably beautiful, and I felt like I could live there forever by myself, away from the pain and drama of the world. Experiencing the sensation that I was one with the universe, I believed that I could touch the stars if I reached out for them. Just as I began to extend my arm, I began to plunge downward. Again I tried to cry out, "Oh, God!" but I was unable to speak. Incredibly, while falling at warp speed, I was capable, somehow, of calculating what would happen to me when I hit my bed while traveling at such an extreme speed. I was absolutely sure my body would shatter into millions of pieces or just vaporize. I prepared myself for impact, and, just before I hit the bed my speed slowed and, like a feather, I gently floated down to the mattress. With my heart pounding uncontrollably, I looked to my right at Maria. Sound asleep, she was both unaware and undisturbed by what I had just experienced!

At that point, I wondered if God had forgotten me. I even had the thought that I was being punished. For some reason my prayers were going unanswered, and I was so tired of it all! Physically and emotionally exhausted, I even pondered the likelihood that I was meant to die at the hospital but that somehow things got messed up. I didn't ask to come back! If I was supposed to die, I wanted to get it over with. I preferred death to continuing down this uncontrollable frightening path. With that final thought going through my mind, I drifted off to sleep.

The following morning, I somehow felt cleansed and renewed, just as I did after my near-death experience in the hospital. My body was tingly with renewed energy, and my emotions seemed balanced and at peace. My feeling was that life would be better for me. I continued to work at my job and did my best to make healthy changes in my life, including staying away from drugs. A part of me felt better because of my efforts to have a normal life again. Maria seemed happier, too. But there still was an underlying inner struggle to understand these spiritual experiences—what they were and why they were happening to me. Where was my life headed?

Massaging my back that evening, Maria said, curiously, "Alex, there's an emerald green colored fluorescent light following the movement of my hands on your back. What is it?"

"They are healing me." I answered her without thinking or understanding where the awareness had come from for me to make such a statement.

"Who is healing you?" Maria asked.

Without hesitation I told her, "Angels are healing me."

Although my answer amused her, she was more interested in investigating the green light. While she massaged my chest, we both noticed the glowing green light wherever her hands moved. The green light had a consistency of translucent gel, intriguing us. We talked for a long time about the light until Maria said she was tired and dropped quickly off to sleep.

As I lay in bed next to her I realized God *had* heard my prayers. I had received a cleansing the night before through my incredible journey to the stars, and that evening I had received a healing by the angels through Maria's nurturing and caring hands.

This seemed to be a turning point for me, and my life started to get a little better. Work became more tolerable, and my relationship with

Maria and her children continued to move forward. I enjoyed being with Maria and her children; I felt they were my own family.

Ahead of me were times I still wanted drugs, especially when my thoughts were of how different I was from everyone else feeling the discomfort of carrying others' pain in me and not knowing what unimaginable out-of-body experience I might have, or when it might happen again. Whenever the temptation to make a phone call to purchase drugs arose, a voice inside me warned, "Alex, you have been given a second chance; do not cause yourself or your loved ones harm." Whenever I heard that warning, instead of purchasing drugs I prayed. Talking to God through prayer took away my focus from escaping my pain through drugs to affirming my desires and asking for higher guidance that I hoped would help me rebuild my life. I felt I had lost my connection to God, and I wanted it back.

Praying is something I did a lot of during this time. I have to admit I didn't always recognize God's signs or pay attention to His higher guidance because of my tendency to get lost and self-absorbed in my inner struggles. My life spiraled downward and became increasingly difficult due to my thoughts, perceptions, and experiences believing that life is unfair, that I had no control over what happened to me, and that others were to blame for my pain. These hopeless attitudes always led to my slipping back into drugs. Following these events I would have brief moments of clarity about the world of misery I was creating for myself. That's when I knew I had to reaffirm my faith with Him. I learned to say over and over again every time I thought life was unfair, "Father, I do not understand, but I move forward with love" with the glimmer of hope that positive change was there for me and that I would discover and become who and what I truly am.

# CHAPTER SIX

# THE LOST YEARS:
# THE DEATH OF MY FATHER

## Fall 1999

Two years after my near-death episode, my father was admitted into the hospital with complications caused by his diabetes; Mom was admitted at the same time after developing pneumonia. During her hospital stay, doctors discovered a large, cancerous tumor on Mom's right kidney.

Although my parents had been in and out of the hospital several times during the previous two years for their various health issues, I felt it was a different story that time for my mother. Her doctors told our family that an operation would be necessary or that she would die from the cancer. After hearing this sad news, I had thoughts about placing my hands on Mom for a healing, but I was still very fearful of the strange, unexplained energy I possessed. Feeling helpless, I prayed to God and asked Him to take care of her. The medication prescribed for Mom cured her pneumonia, and a date was set to remove the tumor.

At that time in my life, drugs were a thing of the past. Without the numbing effects of drugs, I did the best I could to deal with feeling the familiar disconnection from my co-workers and, most recently, from my brothers and sisters. I had also started feeling my siblings' emotional pain whenever I was near them, which was the exact feeling I experienced while in the presence of co-workers. For the first time in my life though, I began to notice how judgmental my siblings were toward each other and toward me.

When Dad returned home from the hospital, I assumed the bulk of responsibility for his care. I was still living at home and worked across the street, so I could check in on him quite easily. Eddie helped as much as he could between his full-time school schedule and part-time jobs. I happily gave Dad's health and recuperation my attention for nearly a month. Then I decided I needed a break. My brothers and sister who lived in town were going to watch over Dad and check in on Mom at the hospital while I took a weekend off to spend time on some personal matters, including seeing Maria. With plans in place, I was comfortable with leaving the house for a breather.

Maria and I were enjoying our Saturday afternoon together when I felt a strong urge to return home to see Dad. I sensed there was something wrong at the house. We quickly drove to my parents' home, where we found my father in his bedroom alone and unconscious, and not one sibling anywhere. I called for an ambulance, and Dad was rushed back to the hospital, where doctors determined he had accidentally over-medicated himself and had been close to dying when Maria and I found him.

I immediately placed a phone call to each of my siblings until one brother answered his cell phone. I learned that they were attending a party and that no one had been with Dad that afternoon. Of course, being totally disappointed in their behavior, I had some very harsh words for them. Distraught at that time about the confusion in my own life, plus my father's overdose and my mother's cancer, I also had to deal with my siblings' irresponsibility toward our parents' well being?! I was emotionally exhausted. I told Maria I had to remove myself from the family drama, and we left the hospital. After driving straight to my parents' home, we packed my things, and I moved in with Maria that night. The situation between my siblings and me continued to worsen, with accusations flying and even harsher words spoken, all of which led to our total distrust of one another. An extremely close family at one time, we were suddenly a broken one.

Putting some distance between my family and me allowed me to see our situation more clearly. I especially did not understand my siblings and felt completely disconnected from them. I was thinking one way, and they certainly were thinking another. I could see how and why it was impossible for us to relate, and I felt we might never again have the relationships we previously shared. I enjoyed living with Maria and her family, but I also mourned the loss of the closeness with my immediate family.

Though I was no longer doing drugs, the desire to escape all the changes in my new life still came on strong. I continued to silently talk to God for strength and guidance during this challenging time. Nevertheless, with the added stress of this latest event with my family, I became worried and anxious about what else might come my way.

Meanwhile, Dad recovered from his overdose and Mom's surgery was a success. Both of them returned home, but sadly my father's health quickly deteriorated once more. At that time, a deep depression settled in on me, and one day I abruptly walked off the sales floor, quitting my job. I felt incapable of handling the drama that came with my new reality and the possible loss of one or both of my parents. Of course, quitting my job created even more drama. With no income, it wasn't long before I ran out of money and had to sell my car. Maria supporting me only added to my unhappiness and made me sink deeper into sadness.

Weeks passed, and my father became severely ill. All the doctors, with all their medicines, were incapable of saving Dad, who I realized had only a few weeks to live. My brothers and one sister ran our parents' household, and on the day of Dad's expected passing they allowed me a five-minute visit with him. Dad's kidneys weren't functioning and his lungs were filling with fluid. I knew it was his time to go, so I had no desire to place my hands on him for a healing. I was not afraid of him dying, because soon he would be where I was not so very long before: the place that we call Heaven. There was a knock on my father's bedroom door, and one of my sisters poked her head in to tell me my time was up. Looking back at my father, I knew this is the last time I would see him alive.

I was heartbroken leaving my father's bedside. Walking across the hallway to my old bedroom I sat dejectedly on the bed. My sister Grace from California wandered into the room. She, too, was looking for solitude—a place to escape from all the activity in the house. Not having seen or spoken to Grace in more than a year, I was aware that she didn't know what was happening in my life. While she sat in a chair facing me, Grace and I exchanged a few brief comments. Soon I found myself confiding in her.

Extending my hands upward in a questioning gesture, I began, "Grace, I don't understand what's going on with me."

Grace's jaw suddenly dropped open and her face turned white as she focused on my hands. "Oh, my God, Alex," she cries. "There are huge beams of white light coming out of your hands!"

Her eyes widened in disbelief at what she was witnessing. She then looked above and beyond my head. "Alex, Mother...." Grace's body trembled as she attempted to finish her sentence, but no more words came out. Grace was quickly freaking me out! Suddenly I began to feel a warm, comforting energy surround me, and an overwhelming sense of peace enveloped me.

Grace finally blurted out, "Mother Mary, Jesus' mother, is right behind you, Alex! White light is coming out of your hands and Mother Mary is standing right behind you with her arms held open!"

Grace's fear and shock suddenly seemed to disappear. She seemed to be in awe, and with amazement in her voice she said, "Oh, she's so beautiful, Alex. She's so beautiful!" Grace then disappointingly said, "She's gone now, Alex" just as I quickly turned my head to see what she was seeing. Unfortunately, I didn't see anything behind me.

Grace and I were silent for a few moments while we just looked at each other, not knowing what to think or say. The event was so surreal, and it had no logical explanation. We both were at a loss for words. Feeling humbled and somewhat overwhelmed by it all, we walked out of the bedroom and into the living room, where we found Maria. After saying our good-byes, Maria and I left. I decided not to tell Maria about that latest happening. Frankly, I wasn't sure she would believe me. Later that evening, one of my brothers called to inform me of our father's passing.

Maria did her best to comfort me as she kissed me on the cheek. Not long after receiving word about my father, I felt a sudden wave of peace come over me. My thoughts immediately went to him that his spirit might have come to say his final good-bye. I didn't say anything to Maria, but I waited to see if I could see his spirit. I waited several minutes but did not see anything, and the feeling eventually faded away.

I could not help looking back through my life with my father. He was an honest, hardworking man who did his best to provide for Mom and all ten of his children. But it wasn't always easy growing up with him. He was raised at a different time, when children were taken out of school to work on farms and any other jobs to help provide an income for their family. He endured the hardship of the Great Depression and fought in World War II. These experiences created an insensitive, hard-shelled man who was unable to express too much love for his children.

Later in his life, though, he became a more gentle and loving man. I remember him asking my mother to please teach him how to pray. I felt this was a way for him to be able to release all the pain he experienced in his life and to be at peace with his God before leaving this world. I loved him tremendously and will forever miss him.

Looking back after all these years, I've had time to reflect on what a blessing it was to be in the small room with Grace as she witnessed the appearance of Mother Mary. Experiencing Mother Mary's presence and her showing herself to my sister was not only to comfort us during the sadness that would soon follow, but also brought to our awareness that she was there to assist in my father's transition to the beautiful and peaceful place where I had been—the place we call Heaven. That event showed me that we are never alone and that we are always loved and supported, especially during our most difficult times.

## CHAPTER SEVEN

# THE LOST YEARS: MY FATHER CONTACTS MARIA

## Fall 1999

Father's funeral was held on a warm, peaceful day in October. Relatives flew in from around the country, and everyone was doing their best to cope with their loss. Understandably, Mom was emotionally numb, having just lost her partner of forty-four years. Dad was the commander-in-chief of our family and the glue that held us together. Whatever he said, we did. Now, with Dad gone, I felt our family faced turmoil, dividing us even further. I sensed that his passing would be the beginning of a different direction for all of us.

During his funeral service, Mother, my siblings, and I had an opportunity to walk up to Dad's casket to say our final good-byes. I already missed him terribly, and when it was my turn I placed a note along the inside of his casket. This was my way of having one last conversation with him. I wrote about how much I loved him and how one day I would see him in Heaven. At the end of the service, each of us family members was given a delicate brass cross by the Catholic priest in memory of my father.

The day after his funeral I received two phone calls from two of my siblings blaming me for our father's death. I was utterly shocked and crushed by their accusations. I felt betrayed and abandoned by my siblings, but with such a large family one can easily imagine the manipulation and dynamics at play: Dad was at home requiring health attention and assistance while two brothers and a sister were at a party, one brother was entrusted with checking in on Dad that day, and yet another brother wasn't even in town on the day of Dad's overdose and a mother who, bless her heart, was in the hospital and would do everything in her power to protect every one of her children to keep the peace. I was ultimately left on the outside looking in. I was the one who found Dad unconscious and left the house to go to Maria's, leaving the drama for everyone else to wheel and deal as they positioned themselves away from responsibility for everything that had occurred that day. Fingers had been pointed at me.

In hindsight, I believe that with all the guilt, grief, and pain they were experiencing at that time, they couldn't see the truth. Instead they needed to vent and point the finger at someone—and I happened to be that someone. I never responded to their accusations. I was deeply hurt, to the point of being heartbroken, but I couldn't respond because I was dealing with my own grief over the loss of my father, and I could not relate to their irrational behavior. I was barely able to handle the drama in my own life because I was still trying to understand the unexplained changes I was experiencing. One thing I was learning, though, was that I was no longer interested in creating drama in my life, and my family equaled drama!

After waking early one morning soon after Dad's funeral, Maria excitedly shared with me an unusual event that occurred while I was asleep that involved the cross that was given to me at my father's funeral. After I returned home from the funeral, I hung the cross on the wall above our bed. Maria said she was awakened during the night by a scraping sound that was coming from the wall above her head. She slowly opened her eyes and saw the cross move up and down, then side to side, for approximately thirty seconds. Excited, I told Maria it must have been Dad's spirit contacting her to say that he was okay. I asked Maria if she was scared, and she said she wasn't. I scanned the room while loudly thanking Dad. I hoped he would appear to us, but he didn't. My father adored Maria, so I was very happy she had that experience with him, though I wished it happened to me, too.

Dad's contact with Maria made me feel better, but my life, in general, worsened by the day. Tension that existed between some of my siblings and me grew even stronger. They even took steps that prevented me from seeing my mother for reasons I couldn't comprehend. This added tension, and the loss of my father led me to a complete loss of hope. I really didn't care about life anymore, and I quickly returned to drugs. I wanted to return to that place of Light and peace—the place where my father now lived.

My relationship with Maria began to disintegrate. Because I was severely depressed, she carried all of our financial responsibility and began having her own struggles with work and her children. She decided to send the children to her parents' home in Fresno, California, in order to protect them from our turmoil. She tried her very best to help because of her love for me, but depression set in for her as well. Though life was becoming increasingly difficult and exhausting, every now and then we would receive signs from Heaven reminding us that we were cared for and watched over.

Returning home from work one night, Maria had an amazing experience: She saw what seemed like hundreds of brilliant white lights flashing on the bedroom wall. She said she was in awe of their brilliance and the peacefulness that emanated from them. I shared my feeling that the lights were angels visiting her to let her know they were there for her.

Years later, after so many of my own experiences, I came to recognize that Maria could see angels and that she was born with the gift of healing, just as I was. It is intriguing to reflect today on my own inability back then to recognize the miracles within and around me, and how they connected me to a larger, magnificent reality. It is so natural for me now, but we were never taught that these things were possible. They do exist, and we all have our own time and way of awakening to who and what we truly are.

# CHAPTER EIGHT

# A MESSAGE FROM HEAVEN

## Summer 2001

Time has a way of quickly passing us by. It wasn't until the summer of 2001, almost two years after my dad's passing, that I would take on a full-time job again. One day I stopped in at a local tobacco shop to chat with the owner, who mentioned, in passing, that one of his employees had just quit. He asked if I would like a job. Almost sure that I could handle selling cigarettes and cigars, I accepted the position and started work the following day.

Although my life remained upside down and I was feeling like a broken man, work slowly brought back some lost self-confidence. I routinely kept in touch with Mom by phone, but I had no contact with my siblings, and I admit that I was feeling lonely. Taking time for prayer helped me to stay away from drugs, for the most part. Maria and I were still together, but our relationship was strained. My inner struggles with my new reality and the notion of having healing abilities was still with me, and the guilt I felt about my inability to be the man I wanted to be for myself and for Maria disheartened me. She had been through so much with me. I had even been praying that she leave me so she wouldn't suffer any longer.

Then, September 11, 2001, a most fateful day, came upon us and the world was witness to terrorist attacks in New York City on the World Trade Center and the tragic collapse of its Twin Towers. Deep fear set in throughout our neighborhood and throughout many other neighborhoods across our great nation. Like so many other Americans, I immediately understood that the world as we always knew it would never be the same. I wondered what would happen next. Was it possible that tragedy could hit near home and affect the two people I cared about most: my mother and Maria?

The world was changing, and while I worked at the tobacco shop on a busy Friday night, my own life changed once again. A man in his mid-fifties walked into the store to purchase clove cigarettes. Hearing his accent, I asked where he originally came from. I learned he was from Australia and worked in international banking. He said that he and a cousin of his from Canada were visiting Arizona and that she was a medium. It must have shown on my face that I had no idea what a medium was, because he explained that she was similar to a psychic, who has the ability to receive impressions of the lives of people past, present, and future. He said that I should see her sometime, and I said I would be interested. With that, we said our goodbyes, and he left.

Shortly after my conversation with the man from Australia, a woman who looked to be in her mid-sixties, was about five feet tall, and had short, gray hair came into the store. With a strong sense of power about her, she briskly walked toward me and stopped. Looking straight into my eyes, she said with graceful authority, "Do not fear. Do not fear. No harm will come to you or your loved ones, so do not fear." I felt my mouth drop open, not only because of her startling statement but because I was feeling that familiar sensation of peace and love—the feeling I experienced while in the presence of Mother Mary.

She continued, "There are a handful of people in this world who control fear and, one by one, they will leave and the world will again be a place of peace and love, so do not fear world events."

I slowly realized she was talking about the recent terrorist attacks, but before I could say anything she looked above my head and continued, "The aura above your head is solid gold, with no cracks or breaks in it. Traveling the world I have seen thousands of people, including those on television who say they can heal, and their auras are not gold like yours. You are one of a handful that I have seen during my lifetime. A gold aura means that you were born with special gifts and God wants to know if you will do His work."

"Yes!" I loudly answered, not realizing or caring that there were customers shopping in the store.

She said, "Good."

Her name was Sheila, and she was adamant that we talk as soon as possible. Taking a deep breath, I hurriedly pondered what that unusual lady was saying and suggested that we meet at ten o'clock the following morning. Sheila handed me a piece of paper with her phone number and address. Leaving, she said, "Alex, it's important."

Without knowing why, but without hesitation, I answered, "I know. I'll be there."

The following morning I nervously drove to the address of an apartment complex Sheila had given me. The neighborhood seemed quiet, and it was not too far from the cigarette store where I worked. After parking my car I walked to the door, where Sheila excitedly greeted me. She invited me inside and asked me to sit down. At that point, I really didn't know what to expect, because I had never been to a medium before. Curious when Sheila asked me to meet with her, I then nervously found myself seated on her sofa.

To explain why she asked me to meet with her, Sheila began, "Alex, last night my cousin returned from the tobacco store and said he met a man with a solid gold aura. There have been only a few people during my lifetime with gold auras at the top of their heads. I knew immediately that I had to speak with you."

"What is an aura, and how can your cousin Rick see mine?" I asked Sheila.

"Rick was born with the ability to see people's energy. Everyone is a vibrational being. Our thoughts, emotions, beliefs, and life experiences create auras of every color of the rainbow, but someone with a solid gold aura like yours is meant to do God's work. You have the ability to heal, don't you?" Sheila asked.

"Yes," I stammered. I was stunned that this woman I had just met knew this about me, and I answered that I had done some healings in the past.

She said, "Alex, your ability to heal will become stronger as you practice your gift." Sheila looked to the right and left of me, then above my head, and said, "Alex, your father is here and he wants me to tell you he loves you very much. He wants you to know that he read the note you put in his casket, and he misses you, too, but it was his time to go. He is the one who moved the cross for Maria that night following his funeral because he wanted her to know that he loved her and would be with her in her life. He thinks of her as a daughter. Alex, he knows you are different from his other children, and he's sorry that they have hurt you so much. He says that you must move on with your life because you have a gift that God gave you and that gift is to help people. Tell your brothers and sisters that he loves them, and let your mother know he misses her and that he's sorry for saying anything that might have hurt her through the years. He says he didn't know what he was saying."

As Sheila told me what my father wanted me to know, my cheeks became wet with tears. "Alex, your father is with his father, mother, and brothers and sisters who crossed over to the other side before him and he's happy and peaceful." Repeating what my dad said, Sheila said, "Son, you must be strong, I love you."

"I love you too, Dad!" I answered. Sheila went on to describe the other family members who were stepping forward and bringing gifts through their messages of love and wisdom. They, too, confirmed that I have the gift of healing. My two grandmothers, a number of aunts, uncles, and a few cousins spoke to me through Sheila, then said goodbye, and left.

Sheila then talked about my future. She said my mother would be on Earth for a while longer because she had some unfinished business with her children. She said the woman I was with loved me but that we would be separated in the future. The angels brought her to me at that time because she was strong and she believed in me. Sheila told me I would be doing healing work for many years to come and that I would travel all over teaching, doing healings, and helping people. Then, she asked if I had any questions. So overwhelmed and dazed by everything that had just happened, I answered, "I don't think so."

Sheila pulled a scrapbook out of a table drawer and opened it to the first page. "That's me, Alex. I was in the movies," she said, pointing to a photo in the book. I had a vague memory of the movie scene of Sheila and the two actors she was showing me. They were all standing behind a crystal ball. I was surprised. She flipped through pages and pages of articles written from all around the world about her and her gift as a medium.

Sheila mentioned that she was in Phoenix to meet with a movie producer friend who has asked for her help. She kindly invited me to stay at her place if I ever visited Canada, where she is quite well known. She assured me that I would have a long line of people to heal if I ever visited.

"I'll think about it," I answered.

After I walked to the front door, we hugged and said goodbye. We promised to stay in touch. "You have my number. I'll always be here for you, Alex," she said.

While thanking her, I said, "I have a lot to think about: who I am, my life, where I'm going." Since that day, however, we have yet to see each other or speak again.

# CHAPTER NINE

# RAINING
# WHITE LIGHT

## Fall 2001

I learned so many things from Sheila that day. Most importantly, I was reminded that there is no such thing as death—at least not as we know it. The detailed information I received from my father and other family members through Sheila helped me understand on a deeper level that, while our physical body may die, our spirit lives on, and our loved ones are still with us. I was particularly grateful to Sheila for my new awareness that healing was real and was a gift, not a curse. She validated the fact that healing would be an inherent part of my future. My life finally seemed to have purpose, but one question still remained: If God chose me to offer healings and help people, why was I experiencing so much turmoil in my life? I still did not have an answer.

A few weeks passed and, just as I suddenly had no longer resonated with my siblings and felt I had to separate myself from them, after my experience with Sheila, who gave me a glimpse of a better life, a similar disassociation from my job and co-workers at the tobacco store presented itself. I learned that there was illegal activity occurring behind the scenes. I was grateful for the work, but I did not want to be associated with or be a part of any such activity, so I left my job, with faith that everything would be okay. Unable to find other work and without a source of income on my part, Maria and I moved from the two-bedroom apartment to a weekly rate, studio hotel room in order to conserve money. At that point, Maria emotionally closed herself off to me. I really couldn't blame her. After all, she loved and cared for me while I was going through difficult changes, and I will be forever grateful to her for saving my life. It seemed that I could only be a source of further disappointment. Again, though, when life seems to become unbearable, miraculous events can take place to support us on our journey.

While Maria was watching television one night, I walked into the bathroom without turning on the light. I closed the door behind me and stood in the dark, feeling only heartache and loneliness. Rain began to fall out of nowhere! Looking up, I saw white light penetrating through the ceiling. Just like during a heavy rainstorm, I felt a light breeze. I could see, hear, and feel rain showering all over me, the sink, the tub, and everything else in the room. I couldn't believe what was happening! I raised my hands into the air above my head to feel the rain of white light on the palms of my hands, and I wondered if it was some kind of sign to let me know that God had not forgotten me. Caught up in the moment, I surrendered myself to God and asked for His help in easing my pain. Moments later, the rain of light stopped and the room became dark again. I waited a few minutes, anticipating what else might happen. I didn't know what to expect, but I knew there was the possibility that I could leave my body. I continued to wait, but nothing happened. A feeling of tremendous exhaustion remained, and yet a glimmer of hope surfaced. I did not tell Maria about this experience. I had been having so many extraordinary experiences at that point, that I was sure she would think I was crazy. I thought it best just to let things be.

The following morning, I woke up feeling peaceful and somehow stronger. I couldn't help thinking about the raining white light and what a magnificent yet bizarre experience it was. What did it all mean? All I knew was that I felt better. Having no idea what my future looked like, I had to believe and have faith that no matter what, my course of destiny would unfold in a very natural way for me.

Interestingly, by the end of that same week, Maria told me she would be moving to Fresno to be with her family. It hurt to hear her say this. In truth, I knew it was the best thing for her. I thought about how difficult a decision it must have been for her, knowing that I did not have anyone else to rely on, or any money to survive.

The following day, I helped her pack her things into her car. Neither one of us spoke very much. After closing the last car door, we stood and looked at each other. That was it. Maria was all I had in life. She was my best friend, and I wanted to tell her how much I loved her and admired her strength, beauty, and heart. But I didn't because I felt it wouldn't mean anything to her anymore. We made a promise to talk to each other often, and I kissed her goodbye.

By the following week, at the age of forty-one, I was homeless. My brothers and sisters did not seem to care, yet ironically I had the feeling that I was cared for because it was just God and me. Off drugs and alcohol, I used whatever money I managed to get from handouts and from Mom for food. I became a humble person during this time. I was newly aware of life itself and everything around me. When families or couples walked past me, I felt their joy. Although I was homeless and missed the feeling of joy for myself, I no longer experienced the constant hopeless feeling that had previously overwhelmed me.

Maria and I talked a couple of times on the phone, thanks to a phone card my mother gave me. She even came down to visit me at my mother's house once. But very soon after, I learned she had a new boyfriend and moved on with her life. I knew I had to do my best to move on with my life, too.

While settled in for another evening in the alleyway I called home, I looked up toward the night sky with its billions of stars and realized how grateful I was to God for just giving me a place to sit.

When people learn about my time living on the streets, they are certain that this was the lowest point in my life. However, I found it to be the source of some of my most peaceful moments. Liberated from all material goods and outside influences, including family, friends, and colleagues, I found that I was able to see the beauty in everything God made, including the beauty within me, and in such simple things like having a place to sit. Through that experience I learned that happiness is within me and I shouldn't require anything or anyone else to "make me happy." What I discovered being homeless and living in an alleyway was a much deeper love for me and for life itself.

# CHAPTER TEN

# THE ROAD TO RECOVERY

## Spring 2002

Waking one morning after a noisy night sleeping in an alleyway, I decided to look up a longtime acquaintance to ask if I could stay with her for a short time. After boarding a bus, I sat on one of the many empty seats near the front and took notice of the bus driver, a man in his late forties who was happily singing gospel songs. He asked how I was doing and said he previously lived in Los Angeles, California before moving to Phoenix. He told me that he became a drug addict while living in Los Angeles and eventually lost his wife, family, and home. One day he realized there was so much misery in his life, he prayed for help. Pulling the bus away from a stoplight, he continued his story, saying that God told him to move to Phoenix, where he would have a better life. Following that advice, he was no longer on drugs, had a good job, and had a special girlfriend who loved him. He emphasized that the only thing he had to do was ask God for help.

While listening to him talk about his good fortune I realized that, like him, I was starting my own journey down the right path. Surely, meeting that bus driver was a sign telling me that I, too, could have a better life. Looking toward Heaven through the bus window, I could feel God's spirit of love, assurance, and support, and I knew that I was ready for positive change in my life.

My friend graciously provided a place for me to stay that evening. The following morning I called my mother and let her know I was okay, because a month had passed since I had last spoken with her. Mom was very happy to hear from me and told me that she loved me. I could hear her concern for my well-being in her voice while she asked me to visit her, saying there was an angel she wanted me to meet. I wanted to see her, too, but I paused before telling her it would have to be some other time, all the while knowing I was disappointing her. She insisted I visit her right away and again said there was an angel waiting to talk with me. My concerns about visiting her were due to the continuing complicated and strained relationships with my siblings. My misgiving was that they would give Mom a difficult time if they found out that I had visited her. While I had this thought running through my head, Mother begged me, "Alex, please come to see me." At that point I knew I could not disappoint her, and I agreed to be at her house within the next several hours.

After taking the bus and walking several blocks to Mom's house, I noticed an unfamiliar car in her driveway. Mom happily greeted me at the door and invited me in. Stepping into the familiar living room, I recognized Father Jorge, an independent Catholic priest from the Shrine of Holy Wisdom. (He's the founder of the center for the study and practice of holistic spirituality.) After we happily and enthusiastically greeted each other, Father Jorge mentioned that it had been a long time since he last saw me.

"Alex, your mother has been telling me about your current situation, and if you can see your way to accepting my help I would like you to stay with me for two weeks," Father Jorge said. Grateful for his wonderful offer, I thanked him and said I would like that. "I spoke with Reverend Jenn, a minister friend of mine, who will take you in for a few weeks following your stay with me," Father Jorge added. Because of their wonderful offers, I was happier than I had been in such a long time. I heard noises, and I turned to see my smiling mother enter the living room carrying two bags of clothing she gathered for my use. Handing them to me, she said, "Alex, God always takes care of us." Lovingly I hugged and kissed her, and replied, "I know, Mom. I know He does." Telling me again that she loved me, she slipped a twenty-dollar bill into my hand. I thanked her for the help.

I enjoyed my two weeks with Father Jorge. Having a clean bed, home-cooked food, and many long conversations during evening hours nurtured my heart and soul. In the mornings, I awoke to the tranquil resonance of Father Jorge chanting in the healing garden behind his home. I was feeling more and more at peace. At the end of two weeks, Father Jorge had made arrangements for me to stay at a local motel for one week with provisions and extra clothing until Reverend Jenn could take me in. When the time came, Reverend Jenn picked me up and we drove to her apartment. I found her to be a pleasant, well-spoken woman, and I guessed she was in her mid-sixties. After I moved the few personal items that I received from my mother and Father Jorge into Reverend Jenn's spare bedroom, we sat down that evening to get acquainted.

"God has plans for you," she said, smiling, while sitting on the sofa across from me. "You're a healer, aren't you?"

"I think so," I answered her. "That's what others tell me."

She patted the sofa cushion next to her and said, "Let me see your hands."

Rising from the chair, I walked over to the sofa, sat down close to her, and held my hands out with my palms facing upward.

After examining my hands closely she said, "Yes, this is where your healing energies come from," pointing toward the center of each palm. "Practice your healings, Alex, and the energies will become much stronger."

"How do you know that I am really meant to heal people?" I asked Reverend Jenn.

She answered, "I know this, Alex, because I am a healer, my mother is a healer, and my grandmother was a healer. When my grandmother passed away several years ago there were hundreds of people, including the then-governor of her home state, who attended her funeral. Mother told me most of them were Grandma's clients. She was a very kind and compassionate woman who helped many people with her healing gift."

Reverend Jenn asked, "What will you do with your gift of healing, Alex?"

I told her I really wanted to help people and she said, "Good." I questioned Reverend Jenn on whether she could teach me about healing. "I can teach you a little, but others will come forward and help you to understand your gift." I promised her that I would do my best, and for the next two weeks I accompanied her while she did healings. She amazed me with her soft, gentle way and internal strength. I watched people get better. She made it possible for me to find the confidence to believe. I learned that it is possible to posses the ability to heal—that it is very real. I also realized during this time that so many people are in need of healing.

Soon I found a job selling professional photography services. Being happily employed with a steady income, I immediately offered to pay Reverend Jenn for room and board. She kindly refused my offer, suggesting that if I saved my money I would have a chance to get my own place to live.

The two weeks with Reverend Jenn passed quickly, and it was soon time for me to move on. I rented a room from a longtime friend, and soon after moving into my new quarters I met a woman who was teaching a healing technique called Reiki. (Reiki (pronounced ray-KEY) means "divine life force energy" and it is a "laying-on-of-hands" technique that arose out of Japanese Buddhism.) I heard, once again, that all things are comprised of energy and that I was blessed with the natural gift to move a tremendous amount of healing energy. I was excited to learn and understand how energy healing works. Within one month I opened a one-room office in Phoenix to begin my practice of energy healing. Along with my practice, I began giving lectures at several family-owned bookstores and organic food stores.

Autumn 2002 quickly settled in, and a local Arizona newspaper printed an article about a holistic healing event I was facilitating. During this event, I met a woman who wanted me to teach a class for her and her friends. I thought the class would be a wonderful opportunity for me. Two months later I began my first class as a teacher. It was exciting for me to find during class that my twenty-plus students were able to feel and move healing energy. I was thrilled! Soon after, I was off to San Francisco to offer more healing sessions and teach another class. Although I was still new to healing and teaching, I found that it came easily and naturally to me. My life seemed to get brighter and more exciting by the day.

# CHAPTER ELEVEN

# A JOURNEY OF PERSONAL HEALING

## Summer 2004

I spent the following year and a half building my skills and confidence in energy healing and experiencing great success in treating clients. My professional life continued to get better, while personally I quietly dealt with the death of my father, the loss of Maria, and the forced separation from my mother. It continued to be an emotional struggle for me, but overall I was happier than I had been in a long time.

In June 2004, I learned that my mother was very ill. I knew in my heart that she didn't have much time to live. The strife between my siblings and me remained. They allowed me to visit her a couple of times in the hospital and once at home before she passed. I miss Mother terribly, but I had a peaceful feeling knowing she was reunited with Dad and her family members in the same place I visited years earlier: Heaven. I learned that my dear mother graciously willed me a small amount of money. This inheritance allowed me to purchase a used vehicle and move into my very own place for the first time in many years. I was so grateful to Mom.

Having my own quiet space gave me the opportunity to become more in tune to my surroundings and myself beyond the physical world. I began to see pinpoints of flashing white lights, and I could see orbs of light for a few seconds at a time. I didn't understand the light orbs and flashes, but I intuitively believed they were angels telling me they were with me. I could sense the presence of my mother and father and, at times, it felt to me that they were together. There were occasions when I would see them for brief moments. When I saw them I was amazed by the peacefulness of their expressions. I began to speak to them practically every day, whether I saw them or not, and was comforted by the fact that they were together and still with me.

Time continued to pass and I began to see larger auras of various colors around clients' bodies while I was working with them. Soon after, I started seeing ethereal bodies with wings that I believed to be angels. It surprised me to find that angels have such huge bodies and are robust like football players. They are so big that their heads touch the ceiling! Their bodies sparkle with light, and I can see right through them. These visions lasted only five to ten seconds before fading away, and I was amazed and humbled by their presence. Whether I saw angels or just sensed them, a loving, tingling warmth enveloped my body when they were around. I experienced the same feeling in the presence of my parents. As a result I never felt alone again.

Working with energies during daily healing sessions with clients, I began to feel my psychic senses awaken, and my body became more sensitive to "subtle" energies. (These are unseen energies that are barely noticeable except to people who are especially sensitive to their surroundings.) I began to comprehend what being "empathic" really meant and why I was capable of perceiving so much more than just the physical world. During this early period of my healing practice, the non-physical world was quickly becoming as real and natural as the physical world was to me.

Having this expanded awareness and sensitivity, I noticed an odd yo-yo effect within myself, creating challenges for me. I had the ability to pinpoint clients' individual problems and create a space of Light, Love, and Healing for them, which I could feel as well. Unfortunately, after leaving the office, that wonderful feeling quickly faded. I became aware of the heaviness of "dense energies," which arose from my own unresolved unhappy memories, worries, and fears.

I wasn't looking for reasons to feel this way. I would walk out of my healing sessions feeling tremendous love and trust in the universe and the direction my life was taking, genuinely grateful for the purposeful work I was doing. But then, unsettling memories and emotions came out of nowhere, popping into my awareness: I remembered the initial trauma from the unanticipated healings of Dulce's baby and my mother's nose, as well as the abrupt out-of-body experiences that created so much fear and turmoil within me, and I wondered if/when it would happen again. I wasn't able to forget the unhappiness my siblings caused my mother, my father, and me. My mind was like a radio transmitter on autopilot sending out scrambled radio signals.

Since my near-death experience on that fateful day at the hospital, I yearned for a life of peace and love, but had been unable to sustain the sensation I experienced while in the Light. It occurred to me that these "dense" energies were weighing me down and not allowing me the chance to experience what I wanted so much for myself: a happier and more loving life.

Then I had an incredible insight: I realized that, like my clients I, too, needed healing. I always wanted to feel good and be happy before my healing sessions, during sessions, and afterward. I no longer wanted to experience the roller coaster ups and downs of emotions, so it was necessary for me to release myself of personal baggage, including past painful events, negative people, and all of those unhappy thoughts and memories that were not loving, nurturing, and supportive.

But the true healing potential was so much more than that. I desired to be healed not only for relief from my personal pain but also because of the deep, inherent wish I had to become a pure channel of Light and love that created healing for my clients. Because I deeply wished for "Heaven on Earth" for my clients, too, I surmised that my being the best *I* could be had to benefit them that much more. Perhaps their disease and pain would even be able to dissipate faster!

While contemplating how I might accomplish this, I became excited about my theory. Thinking through the possibilities, I wondered why I couldn't turn the tables and give healing energies to myself. Would that be possible? I wondered. When clients received healing energies from me they began to feel so much better. Would it work if I did the same thing to myself?

While relaxing in bed one evening, I was remembering my experience in Heaven, understanding that we are beings of Light and that we all are a part of God's great love. I recalled understanding that all emotional, mental, and physical disease is due to the lack of light. And with that, I found myself placing my hands over the center of my chest and said silently, "*I now bring in Light, Love, and Healing. I now bring in Light, Love, and Healing.*" I concentrated on my heart, because I wanted to relieve it of the grief and pain that had become my partner. I felt some warmth first in my head, and then it traveled down my body and out into my hands, causing them to tingle. The warmth receded from my hands, entered my heart, and then slowly expanded throughout my entire body. I repeated the Light, Love, and Healing statement again and again, and over again.

Within a few minutes a sense of peace came over me. I experienced a deeper understanding of who I was and where my life was headed. As my body relaxed, simple thoughts of gratitude filled my awareness. I was grateful to be alive and to have my own place to live, and that my clients were healing. How incredibly relieved and thrilled I was to find that by simply bringing the three nurturing energies of Light, Love, and Healing into my own body, I was able to begin transforming how I felt and thought!

I continued to bring Light, Love, and Healing into myself three times a day like clockwork, with the final healing taking place just before going to sleep at night. It was comforting to know that my last thought before falling asleep was that I am Light, Love, and Healing. With each passing day I felt more peaceful within myself and was more satisfied with what I had in life. People mentioned how peaceful and happy I looked to them. Some of the painful memories from my past that normally plagued me had diminished considerably within one month's time. Others, I believed, needed more work. It became a ritual for me to bring in Light, Love, and Healing whenever I had a negative thought or memory until I felt better.

As the weeks passed, I continued to feel more at peace and more joyful, and I was able to sustain a greater amount of healing energies for longer periods of time. Being the impatient guy that I am, though, I continued to search for a technique that would decrease the time it took me to heal myself and others. Soon after this thought, I was introduced to meditation, a process of sitting quietly to reach a deeper state of peace and awareness. While meditation seemed wonderful to me, I learned that some people had to practice it for months or even years before they are able to sustain an emotional and/or physical balance in their daily lives. Most of my clients and students wouldn't have that kind of time to spare, and most people want to be free of heartaches and heartbreaks as soon as possible. So, my newest quest was to discover a way for my clients to be at peace *now*!

# CHAPTER TWELVE

# A BREAKTHROUGH

## Winter 2004

Channel surfing as I looked for something to watch on television during the December holiday season, I found a movie I had seen many times as a child. In the movie, Jesus was on the cross and as He looked up to Heaven He said, *"Forgive them, Father; for they know not what they do."* This scene brought home the realization that we were all doing the best we could with our lives. I, too, was doing the best that I could with mine.

Relating this "epiphany" to my own life, I realized I had been too harsh with myself for making poor decisions like drinking excessively and doing drugs to escape my fears, and for continuing to carry so much guilt about hurting Maria and her children. Also, I wasn't able to forget the unfairness of my siblings' behavior toward me. My siblings, I realized, didn't know how to do better, because they were still learning. Fundamentally, they were doing their best each moment in time. How could I judge anyone, including myself, when we are all just learning? It became clear to me that "forgiveness" on my part ultimately would relieve the remaining pain in my heart and in my life. *And I wanted it.*

I closed my eyes and said aloud, *"I forgive myself for causing myself pain through my thoughts, words, and actions, for I am just learning. I now forgive every man, woman, and child for causing me pain through their thoughts, words, and actions, for they are just learning."* After I took a deep breath and exhaled, memories of some of the most painful moments of my life appeared clearly in my mind. As these thoughts surfaced, I became emotional and teary-eyed. My body then vibrated slightly, and when I repeated the forgiveness statement I felt energy building within me that quickly turned into a heaviness tightly wrapping itself around my chest. My emotions and heart ached for relief. After repeating the same statement for a third time, the tightness gradually loosened its grip and began to move through my upper torso, out toward my shoulders, along my arms, and finally into my hands. Concentrating intensely, I shook my hands vigorously in an attempt to remove the dense energy out and away from me. I focused on the heaviness that had traveled down into my legs, and I felt it escape my body by taking a path out through my feet, perhaps similar to a stream of water flowing.

After a slight muscle spasm I began to feel lighter and lighter in both my emotions and in my physical body as the heaviness escaped. Fully engaged in the experience, I suddenly realized a buildup of dense energy was occurring in one of my legs. Concentrating as hard as I could, I attempted to break up the clogged energy in that leg, but I was unable to do it! My leg was feeling extremely uncomfortable. I tapped my foot with a finger while imagining it was a magnet pulling clogged energy from my leg out of my foot. While doing this, I repeated the forgiveness phrase one more time and was surprised to feel the clog break apart. After the energy releasing was finished I felt much better, clear-headed, relaxed, and fifteen pounds lighter!

Without a doubt, forgiveness has been one of my most therapeutic experiences, and it changed my perspective on so many things. By forgiving others, and myself, I was able to release the energy that created my most deeply rooted issues.

After my first forgiveness episode, I perceived happenings usually upsetting to me in a different light. I no longer felt hurt or angry about past events. I felt compassion for everyone and became supportive of where we all were in our life's journey. It became apparent to me that

I needed to be kinder to others and to myself, and I no longer cared so much about what other people thought or said. Most importantly, I was able to recognize who I was and decided to be the best person I could be in order to bring Light, Love, and Healing to as many people as possible. No longer possessing the need to judge anyone or anything was incredibly liberating!

Through forgiveness, the negative energies within me shifted to positive ones. When my energy body changed, I noticed that my thoughts automatically changed for the better, too. As my thoughts changed, my whole life changed. My perspective about life and the world shifted, and I began to notice positive change in my practice of energy healing. My intuition expanded and provided me with the ability to sense clients' emotional and physical conditions. This new ability allowed me to focus attention on specific, affected areas of the body and send healing energies directly to only those areas. Healing energies surged easily through me and more powerfully into my clients. I could sense when they might benefit from the forgiveness process, and I led them through a guided meditation to assist them in healing their ailments.

Nancy is one client who benefited from the process of forgiveness. Let me share her story to illustrate how well it works and how life-changing it can be for clients. When Nancy first visited my office, she told me that she was in her mid-forties and that she had been diagnosed years earlier with fibromyalgia, a medically recognized illness that causes chronic body pain. Nancy had lived with her pain for many years and, as a last resort, she was referred to me with the hope that I would be able to help her. When I entered the treatment room I couldn't help but notice Nancy's quietness as she sat on the treatment table.

After the usual introduction, I explained to Nancy how the process of energy healing works. (I do this by using a comparison to everyday things. I learned along the way that clients get a better and quicker grasp of what to expect when the technique is explained to them in this manner.) Methodically I explained that the human body is similar to a computer and that the body consists of billions of intelligent, interacting cells that are conscious, listening and reacting to everything we think, say, and do. Information is downloaded into us from the moment we are born. Genetics and a lifetime of experiences get absorbed into our bodies and are put into the memory of these billions of cells. Some of our stored information is positive and nurturing, like love, joy, peace, and gratitude. Other information is negative and non-nurturing, like heartbreak, fear, shame, and guilt. When the cells of our body absorb too much negative emotional information they become overwhelmed and unable to function properly. The result is emotional distress and then physical disease. Stress is a negative emotion that attacks the nervous system, vascular system, heart, and other major organs of the body. Stress and other negative forces can eventually cause physical disease and possibly death. I told Nancy, as I tell all my clients, that my purpose was to assist her in the release of negative cell-stored information and ultimately fill that empty space with a new program: Light, Love, and Healing. Having the healing process explained in simple terms helped Nancy better understand. She said she was comfortable enough to proceed.

It was quite evident that Nancy was in pain as she tried to lie down and get into a comfortable position. As she reclined on the table, I lightly supported her back with my hand. After she settled into a relaxed position, I closed my eyes and took a deep breath. With my hands on my chest I began silently saying, *"I now bring in Light, Love, and Healing."* After my body was charged with nurturing energies, I opened my eyes and asked Nancy if she was ready. I told her, "I will tap an energy point on your body one time and your negative energy will begin to flow out from that point, and after I will send you Light, Love, and Healing."

Nancy closed her eyes, and I said, "Repeat after me: I now forgive myself for causing myself pain through my words and actions, for I am just learning. I now forgive every man, woman, and child for causing me pain through their thoughts, words, and actions, for they are just learning." Nancy softly repeated the words and I felt energy begin to flow out of her body. Opening her eyes, she stared intently at the ceiling, and I asked her to repeat the healing words a second time. I noticed a teardrop had formed in the corner of her left eye and began to run down her cheek. For a period of five minutes Nancy forgave various people she felt had created some kind of pain in her life.

Again I asked Nancy to repeat after me: "I now release all my physical and emotional pain." I had a sensation of tiny needles on the index finger I had placed on Nancy's body to remove the dense energies creating her pain. Quickly these energies were released from Nancy. She took a deep breath, exhaled, and continued to repeat the phrase over and over during the next ten minutes. After feeling that Nancy's body had finished releasing the dense energies, I began to send the energy of Light, Love, and Healing to her by placing both of my hands four to five inches in the air above her body. A wonderful, warm energy radiated within me, and for the next twenty minutes it flowed out of my hands and into Nancy.

Gently touching Nancy on her left hand, I asked how she was doing. She said, "Alex, while I was forgiving my family and myself I felt what I would call a heavy darkness being pulled from the area where your finger was on my body. When I repeated 'I now release all of my physical and emotional pain,' I could feel the pain leaving my body. Then when you placed your hands over me I closed my eyes and saw a white light and it felt as if I was floating several inches above the table. Alex, I feel pain free!"

I then asked Nancy to place both hands on her chest and repeat after me: "I now bring in Light, Love, and Healing," and I followed with instructions for her to take a deep breath and exhale. She did this several times before opening her eyes and smiling. I knew by her reaction that she was feeling the warm energies. I suggested that she bring in Light, Love, and Healing energies three times each day in five-minute durations in order to reprogram her cells to *be* Light, Love, and Healing. Nancy assured me she would follow my instructions. As she left the office she appeared to be at peace and full of hope. I never heard from Nancy after that day.

Forgiveness has been such a powerful healing tool for both my clients and me. It facilitates the release of emotional pain from our memories and provides the opportunity and ability to fill that empty space with Light, Love, and Healing. Once I made this connection that new energies could take the place of harmful ones with forgiveness, I became extremely excited and hopeful that I might be able to help so many others this way. Another fascinating idea came to me soon after experiencing my forgiveness revelation. I asked myself, *"Why not assist my clients in releasing the same negative attributes from them that I had so badly needed released from myself?"* I went to my desk and quickly listed ten items that immediately came to mind. Checking my appointment book, I learned that my next client's name was Sue.

While greeting Sue, I noticed that she was perhaps in her thirties and was an attractive woman who appeared particularly tired and drained. I began to experience a strong tightness around my heart and a shortness of breath. (These feelings tell me what my client is experiencing.) Sue took a seat on top of the treatment table and informed me she was married, had two children, and had been struggling with several fears that had completely taken control of her life over the past ten years. After she finished her story, I explained that I could help her body release old, non-serving thoughts and memories. Sue quickly replied, "I'll do anything you say. I've been so depressed and afraid most of my life. I have been to so many doctors who have been unable to help me. My husband, my children, and I are hoping you can help." I told Sue that I would do my best and asked her to lie down, close her eyes, and try to relax.

Removing the list of ten negative attributes from my desk and placing it on top of the table next to me, I positioned my hands across my chest to bring in Light, Love, and Healing. As I did with Nancy, I placed a finger near the energy point on Sue's body and tapped once where she would release. I ask Sue to repeat after me: "I now release from every cell of my body, my heart, and mind all confusion..." and, before she had a chance to repeat the statement, I could feel the negative energy start to flow out of her body! Surprisingly her body began releasing the first negative attribute on the list before she asked it to. We move on to the next attribute on the list: "I now release doubt...." This time a small amount released and I moved on to the next attribute: "I now release worries...." Immediately, a huge surge of energy began to flow out and diminished after a minute. After doing *worries,* I moved to *anger.* Not much released with *anger.* The next attribute on the list was *stress,* but before I could speak the word out loud, negative energy started to flow out of Sue. I decided not to ask Sue to repeat any of the attribute words after experiencing such a surprising response. By that time, I was sure my energies were somehow connected to her energies and I would only have to use my thoughts to pull out her negative attributes. Sue quietly slept during the next five minutes while I continued to assist her in releasing the negative emotions remaining on my list: *shame, grief, fear, judgment,* and *heartbreak.* After completing the list of attributes, I sent Sue Light, Love, and Healing for twenty minutes.

When I gently touched Sue's hand to awaken her she startled me with a really big smile! Her eyes were sparkling and the darkness under them had faded; she was glowing. Sitting upright, Sue looked around the room, down at her hands and feet, and then at me. She said, "Alex, I feel like I have just awakened from an awful, ugly nightmare because everything seems so bright and beautiful!"

By allowing herself to release dense non-nurturing energies like fear, worry, and shame, Sue was able to raise her energy vibration to a higher state of being almost immediately. She was now experiencing the world at a more nurturing and higher perspective, and that higher perspective is a place of peace, joy, and love. As I helped Sue off the table and onto her feet she promptly gave me a hug and thanked me.

We just smiled and looked at each other for a moment until I finally said, "Sue, go and have fun with life!" We shared a wonderful laugh together. While I walked Sue to the door, she thanked me once again.

As I reflect upon the healing of Nancy, Sue, others, and myself, I know that, after all this time, I have found what I was looking for: a simple, yet powerful technique to assist in obtaining a faster healing physically and emotionally raising my clients' vibration to a higher consciousness. I had the capability to take negative non-nurturing energy, replace it with nurturing positive energy, and provide clients an escape from anxiety, stress, worries, fear, confusion, and physical pain! Greater clarity and peace of mind can be achieved with this technique, as well as relief from the usual symptoms of migraine headaches, backaches, heart disease, tumors, depression, and more. Clients often mention after their sessions how they are able to feel dense energies leave their bodies. They also feel a sense of peacefulness enter their bodies in its place. Some clients experience a floating sensation. Others see various waves of colored lights, orbs of flashing light, and even angels and other heavenly beings.

With a passion in my heart to help people, and with love as my guide, I continue to use the "release-and-bring-in" technique with clients. The technique allows simple, quick, and effective healing results—faster than any prior healing process I knew. I was my own guinea pig, so to speak, when I discovered this technique, so I was certain I could teach people to use it on themselves or their loved ones.

On a personal level, I shifted my own energies from unbalanced to balanced. Balancing my energies changed my thoughts, which ultimately led to changing my life. I transitioned from harboring almost constant uncertainty to entrusting that everything is perfect just by gaining a new perspective about the world and me. I learned that each and every person and event in my life served a higher purpose and had brought me to where and who I was. Waking each morning I was just happy to be alive, and I truly looked forward to what new experiences each day might bring. I felt better about my life than I ever did before. Situations or people that previously bothered me seemed to bounce off me like a small, flat rock thrown just the right way skips across water. I began to release anything from my body that might hang over me like a dark cloud and replaced it with Light, Love, and Healing to raise my energy vibration into a higher state of consciousness. Finally! It felt like, once again, I had a direct connection to the Light, love, and wisdom of Heaven. By sustaining this joyful state, life opened its doors and brought me greater information, wonderful people, and new opportunities. My life and healing technique moved forward in unexpected ways. Yet, this was just the beginning of what would soon unfold for me and my life's work!

# CHAPTER THIRTEEN

# "THE HAPPY HEALER"

## Winter 2004

During the latter part of 2004, clients began to tell me they could feel, hear, or see angels at times during their energy healing sessions with me. Because of my own experiences, I knew their angels were very real. I learned to call upon these powerful beings of light for assistance with healings. Around this time a friend told me about a woman, Char Mada, who was teaching a course on communicating with angels and, with my desire to gain a better understanding of them, I decided to take her class.

Char lectured in class about the connection we have with each other, whether we are living in a flesh body or in spirit, like angels. I learned a very important fact about healing in this class: Because humans are electrical bodies created from the same source of Light in Heaven, the energy we call God, clients would be capable of receiving healing energies from me even if we were in different locations. And that is how miracles happen for another when we pray for them. As it turned out, this teacher and the information she shared would allow me to take my healing work to a much broader audience than I ever had before.

After completing the course on communicating with angels, Char invited me to be a guest on her Internet radio talk show, "Charmed Angel Talk" (on www.achieveradio.com). Char said that listeners from around the world phoned into her talk show every Wednesday night to request messages from angels. I wasn't sure I would be able to provide her listeners with messages, but I thought I would be able to help by sending healing energies to her listeners. Thinking the talk show would be a great opportunity for me to work on long distance healings, I made my media debut.

As listeners called into the radio show to ask Char and her co-host for messages from angels, I simultaneously tuned into callers' energies and sent them Light, Love, and Healing. I was surprised that I could easily feel their energies at such long distances. Char asked for my input with callers, and I explained on air the different energies coming from each caller to me. I asked callers if they wanted to release their emotional or physical pain, or any other barriers that prevented them from having happier, healthier, and more loving lives. With their permission I guided them through the Mastery of Energy Healing "I now release" process I so happily developed.

Limited to a five-minute time constraint with callers, this radio work required my quick focus and attention on the negative attributes that needed to be released from each particular person. For example, if my heart felt severe pain I assisted the caller in releasing grief, heartaches, and heartbreaks. I extended my right hand away from my body into mid-air, as if it was gently lying above the caller's heart, and I sent Light, Love, and Healing until the pain in my own heart dissipated. A feeling of peace flowed through me, and callers simultaneously responded by saying they felt various sensations run through their bodies. These sensations included tingling feelings, heat, calmness, peace, lightness in the chest area, a visualization of colors, and/or relief of physical pain. After completing my first two-hour show with Char, the radio station owner asked if I would be interested in hosting my own show once a week at the station. He explained that people who needed help could call in to request healing energies. I excitedly accepted the invitation.

Just weeks later "The Happy Healer" show was born. I featured guest authors, professional speakers, and doctors who shared their wisdom about healing during the one-hour show. Other shows I dedicated to sharing my experiences about Heaven and the after-life, as well as why we need to forgive, how to live a life free of judgment, fear, and ego so we all can live "Heaven on Earth." Listeners throughout the United States and Canada and around the world called to request healings for themselves or their loved ones. Migraine headaches, back pain, heartache, depression, tumors, and cancer were just some of the emotional and physical ailments callers wanted released. The show helped me improve my long-distance healing skills, and I enjoyed receiving quick, positive confirmation of the effect of each healing. Most callers felt a significant reduction of discomfort or physical pain. A small percentage said they felt nothing.

I encouraged callers to actively participate in the healing process. Many were unaware that the world and they were made of energy. I asked them to place their hands one inch apart in front of their bodies, with palms facing toward each other, and slowly attempt to pull their hands away to *feel* the energy existing between them. They were often astonished when they felt a tingling or a taffy-pulling-like energy between their hands. I then asked callers to hold their hands six inches apart and imagine themselves moving a ball of energy from the palm of their left hand to the palm of their right hand, back again to the left hand, and so on. Many were extremely surprised that they could feel energy. To empower some callers, I asked them to extend one hand outward, in a position similar to a traffic officer stopping traffic, and send Light, Love, and Healing to loved ones or beloved animal companions. After experiencing the flow of healing energy through their hands, they quickly changed their negative thoughts and feelings of helplessness, and realized that everyone possesses the gift of healing.

Anyone can be in a state of healing and share it with others; therefore, anyone can do what I do. It is our God-given right to experience

Heaven on Earth. When people shift their thoughts and emotions of fear, anger, and judgment toward themselves and others to thoughts and emotions of Light, Love, and Healing, they create a higher and more pure energy vibration of themselves, which expands outward to their surroundings. Jesus, Buddha, Mother Theresa, and Gandhi have proven this well as they walked upon the Earth emanating humility, compassion, and love. They were able to bring healing to the sick and more peace to humanity. You can do this also. (Exercises that you can do to nurture and bring healing to yourself and others can be found in Appendix A.)

Many factors can cause people to not heal. For example, they have not yet completely opened up to receive the healing energies, or they may be experiencing unworthiness of being healed or have been ill for so long that they have completely given up all hope. In these instances, their negative thoughts and emotions block the healing energies from being received. In other cases, there is a higher purpose behind the illness at a soul level. For those who simply do not *feel* the healing energies within their physical body, it does not mean that the healing is not received physically, emotionally, mentally, or spiritually. It simply means that their physical body is not sensitive to these subtle energies at this time, for we are constantly changing and evolving, are we not? The more one becomes aware of the different energies and works with them, the more sensitive he or she will become to sensing these subtle energies.

During one radio show, Randy Benowitz, a jeweler from Chicago, called in and asked me to send Light, Love, and Healing to her mother. Randy's mother was in a Minnesota hospital suffering from severe abdominal pain caused by intestinal scar tissue built up from a previous surgery. Because I could feel the heat of the energy flowing from my hands, I felt Randy's mother received the healing energies over the air. Randy shared her response on the telephone that she intuitively also felt her mother's healing.

Off the air, I provided Randy with my personal phone number and asked her to call and update me on her mother's condition. The following evening Randy called to say that her mother's pain had diminished dramatically but that she was still in the hospital waiting for her intestines to work normally. Randy provided me with additional details about her mother that helped me connect more directly with her mother's energy. I began by sending healing energy to her mother's stomach. As I slowly worked through the intestinal tract, Randy interrupted me and said she could actually see in her mind a white energy moving through her mother's intestines. She described her mother's intestinal tract as being blocked in some areas like a bent straw. I asked Randy to assist me, and we mentally moved through her mother's intestines, untwisting and unblocking them. After thirty minutes of healing, we both agreed that her mother's blocked areas were open. Randy said she would again update me on her mother's condition the following day.

The next day, as promised, Randy called to inform me that her mother's condition was again much improved. After five days in the hospital, she was being released. The following evening, her mother was feeling well enough that she attended a dinner party and three days later flew to California to visit family. Grateful for my help, Randy invited me to Chicago to teach a class on my Mastery of Energy Healing technique (M.E.H.).

Months later, I found myself in Chicago. Randy gathered a group of her friends and others interested in the healing arts. Each paid an affordable fee to take my class at a location that Randy secured. This scenario quickly became typical of how I received lecture, private healing, and teaching opportunities.

Julie George, another Happy Healer Show caller, asked for my assistance with releasing the sinus headaches she suffered from for several years. I worked with her on the releasing process for not quite four minutes, after which she excitedly said her sinus headache had all but disappeared. A few weeks later Julie called me requesting help for her son, who was suffering from kidney stones. His doctors recommended surgery after he had experienced severe pain and bleeding off and on for several days. I sent Julie's son Light, Love, and Healing energies, and I received a phone call from her telling me that her son's pain was gone and that surgery would not be needed. She was so excited with her son's results that she asked me to do a lecture, teach a class, and give individual healing sessions in her hometown of Erie, Pennsylvania. I agreed to go to Erie.

Julie coordinated everything for me. She put an advertisement in the local newspaper, and set up an evening lecture and healing meditation at a nearby conference facility, as well as three days of private healing sessions and a Mastery of Energy Healing class held during one weekend day. The one ad attracted about fifty people for the lecture, we filled our private healing session appointments, and we had about twenty individuals attend the class.

I thoroughly enjoyed the opportunity to reach out through Internet radio and help people who lived in other parts of the country, but I continued to search for opportunities to inspire local Arizona listener involvement as well. One day I received a call from my friend Soleil, who runs a horse rescue ranch called the Arizona Equine Rescue Organization in Scottsdale, a suburb of Phoenix. Her ranch has a program that assists people who are dealing with emotional trauma and physical disease, giving them an opportunity to work with, or just be around, horses. Their program provides the tools to help people acknowledge their inner spirit and in turn promote good health and well-being.

Soleil told me about Glen, a man involved in her rescue program who was suffering from severe heart disease. She gave me his phone number, and I called him to arrange an appointment. The next day Glen knocked on my door. While introducing myself, I observed Glen's declining posture and felt an overwhelming sense of fatigue and despair emanate from him.

After taking a seat just outside the healing room, Glen said he had dealt with heart disease for a number of years. After enduring four heart attacks, he underwent quadruple bypass heart surgery. In 2003, his doctors' prognosis was that he would suffer a fatal heart attack within one to two years. He even participated for one year with experimental stem cell therapy at the National Institute of Health in Bethesda, Maryland. On oxygen and for the most part confined to an electric scooter, Glen was taking thirty-two different prescription medications each day, including eighteen to nineteen pills just for his heart and four pills for depression. He also took up to sixteen nitro-glycerin pills daily for heart pain.

I could sense his anguish and depression. Staying calm and positive, I told Glen I would do my best to help him and then, for some unknown reason, I told him a joke. Glen laughed and reciprocated with a joke of his own, which made us both crack up laughing. I told him a second joke, and he followed with another joke. The joke telling went on until I realized that twenty minutes had quickly passed!

"Well, Glen," I said cheerfully, "let's see if we can help you," as I motioned for him to follow me to the room where I do my healing work. A half hour later he walked out of the room able to see the beauty in the world for the first time in three years. Seeing Glen to the door, he expressed happiness, and his eyes had new life. We set an appointment for the following Tuesday.

When he returned the following week, Glen's mood was much brighter, and he shared some positive news: His depression had completely left him, but the chest pain and breathing difficulties still troubled him. We sat and told a couple more jokes, then went into the healing room to work. Glen was so relaxed during his second session that he actually fell asleep.

When we finished, I asked how he felt. Glen looked around the room and hesitantly answered, "Fine," and took a deep breath. His body began to relax as the breath he took in, without his oxygen tank, began to work. It was the first time in many years that he could get enough oxygen breathing without assistance. Color had come back into his face, and he smiled.

Glen called me the next week to share some exciting news. He and his wife had always loved dancing. Three days after his second visit, they went ballroom dancing, where he reported they danced for two and a half hours, resting for only fifteen minutes. Ironically, this time it was Glen's *wife* who got tired! We laughed. He said he had taken no nitroglycerin pills for heart pain since his second visit and would begin weaning himself off his medications, which would eventually leave only one pill a day to manage his diabetes. He could easily walk over a mile and a half each day without discomfort. He no longer required oxygen to assist his breathing, and he never used his scooter again.

Glen's cardiologist was stunned. Follow-up tests revealed no evidence of Glen ever having heart disease.

Because Glen's was an extraordinary story of healing that could provide hope to others who were ill, I asked if he would consider sharing his story with The Happy Healer Show listeners. He said he would love to share his story. I decided the show featuring Glen would be called *"What About Glen?"* Glen came to the radio station the following Tuesday. With great courage and, at times, tearful eyes, he told listeners about his journey from hopelessness and despair to emotional, mental, and physical recovery. The show was such a success with listeners that I invited several other clients to be on the show to tell their personal stories. Clients eagerly told stories of healings from migraine headaches, strokes, and cancer. Some were stories told by people who had, at one point, been at death's doorway. They happily gave others a message of hope and reminded listeners that they should never give up, regardless of how hopeless a situation seems.

The *"What About...?"* series continue to be some of my most successful shows mainly because they help listeners let go of their fears and any feeling of unworthiness, and allow them to heal. Just by telling his story, Glen had a healing experience. Over time my radio show went through a transformation, changing from a guest-driven show to one highlighting individuals with personal healing stories. I believe my purpose in life, including my job as a radio show host, is to remind as many people as possible that we all are beings of love. By "being" love we can help not only our own selves heal from past hurtful experiences, we can also help each other. Love is the most powerful, creative energy in the universe. Through love, anything is possible!

# CHAPTER FOURTEEN

# LECTURES AND HEALING MEDITATIONS

## Summer 2005

A number of my Internet radio show listeners began to invite me to lecture and teach my Mastery of Energy Healing technique around the country. One destination that I mentioned previously was Erie, Pennsylvania, during the summer of 2005. I looked forward to lecturing at the beautiful conference facility that sat peacefully along the banks of Lake Erie. The grounds held an abundance of beautiful trees when I arrived, bushes and flowers were in bloom, and the weather couldn't have been more perfect.

Standing in the doorway greeting new arrivals who hoped to be healed of their emotional distress or physical disease, I began to sense the energies, thoughts, emotions, and physical pain of those who came to listen. More than 100 attended from all walks of life. Among those in the audience were teachers, doctors, yoga instructors, students, and homemakers. Some were married and others single; some were young and some old. I was determined to do my best to help every lecture attendee. My one-on-one healing appointment schedule was booked solid.

After everyone settled in for the lecture, I walked to the front of the room and looked into each person's face. Everyone looked so beautiful as they sat or stood in silence, and I deeply hoped they would all be healed. Closing my eyes I began to meditate, "I *am* Light, Love, and Healing. I *am* Light, Love, and Healing...." As is usually the case, I began to experience a tingling sensation, and then a powerful energy expanded throughout my body and into the crowd. The energies increased even more as I asked God and the angels for help. A few minutes passed, but it seemed much longer because real time slowed down, like it did with Dulce's sick baby in that small Mexican border town long before.

Greeting the group after taking a deep breath, I began the story of my life—how I was just a normal guy, and suddenly one day, many years before, my life drastically changed when a friend handed me her dying baby and somehow the child was healed. I shared with them the story of my near-death experience and that there is no death, only a new beginning.

I explained, "From the moment we are born, we begin to absorb information about our life into our heart, our mind, and every cell of our body. It's called 'cell memory.' Some information we absorb is nurturing and positive in nature, such as joy, peace, gratitude, and love. Other information is non-nurturing and negative in nature, such as grief, anger, judgment, and heartbreak. When we accumulate enough of the lower energies, emotional distress sets in, followed by physical disease."

Looking around the tightly packed room I saw heads nodding up and down with understanding. "We *are* our life experiences. So, the question is: Can we release negative energies from ourselves, just as we delete old information from a computer in order to bring in new, positive information and energies? Sure we can, because I have done it! And as you bring in this new, positive information and energy, a person can heal emotionally, mentally, physically, and spiritually. Every one of you can do it today if you want. Is everyone ready?" A loud "yes" filled the room and I responded to their answer with, "Good. Let's begin."

The room became totally silent in anticipation of what might follow. I asked the audience to close their eyes and place both hands in their laps, palms facing upward. Because of my faith I was aware that whatever happened next was the result of knowing how to "let go and let God." I existed only as a messenger to remind people that we are love. As that thought and energy filled me, I asked the group to repeat after me: "I now release…." I led everyone through the Mastery of Energy Healing releasing process and asked them to place their hands on their chests to bring in Light, Love, and Healing energies. Reacting in various ways, some participants quietly cried, others sighed, some took deep breaths, some experienced slight twitching, and some seemed so peaceful I felt they were in a state of bliss.

After a twenty-minute meditation, I asked them to open their eyes and acknowledge if they experienced negative energies leaving their bodies. Half the audience quietly replied they had, and half of the participants just nodded their heads, signifying they had. Many hands reached into the air when I asked if anyone wanted to share his or her experience with the group. One by one they each described the different aches and pains that were released through various places on their bodies. Some reported visions of past events or people they felt were responsible for the pain released from their bodies. Others reported they saw loved ones who had transitioned to the other side, angels, or other heavenly beings.

Moving on to the next step, I asked everyone to close their eyes, put one hand out in front of them like a traffic officer stopping traffic, and send Light, Love, and Healing energies to a loved one or someone who might need help. Almost everyone reported feeling energy being pulled out of his or her hands and believed that it was absorbed by the person he or she chose. After everyone put their hands back in their laps, I continued, "From this moment forward, bring Light, Love, and Healing into yourself and send it to others daily. By doing this, you are bringing into your consciousness, your heart, and every cell of your body the energy of Light, Love, and Healing, and you will become it, giving the opportunity for others to become it also."

One woman questioned, "Alex, does it actually work?" I replied with a question back to her: "If you were sick in a hospital, would you want your family members and friends to send you thoughts of fear and hopelessness, or would you prefer they send you thoughts of Light, Love, and Healing?

She quietly replied, "I would want them to send me Light, Love, and Healing."

I continued, "That's right, because intuitively, we know that love heals. It is the most powerful creative energy in the universe. When emotional and physical disease sets in, it is due to the lack of Light. The Light holds the energies of love, peace, joy, healing, and all that is nurturing. So when we send Light, Love, and Healing, it is reawakened in cells of the body, and that is how healing occurs. That was the information given to me in Heaven."

After answering their questions for a half hour, I thanked the audience for coming to my lecture. People slowly left their seats, and a crowd began to gather around me while I made my way toward the doorway, where I planned to stand and personally thank everyone as they exited the room. A woman in her fifties excitedly told me she suffered for more than twenty years from severe lower back pain and, for the first time in years, she didn't feel any more pain! I cheerfully said, "I love you" to her. She replied with, "I love you too, Alex" as she walked through the doorway.

Another woman in her mid-thirties stopped at the door to say her mother had died years earlier and, after she heard me say my journey to Heaven was such a beautiful, peaceful, and loving experience, she finally felt she could let go of the pain she still felt from losing her mother. Thinking that she would be able to move on with her life, this woman also felt she could share today's experience with family members and help them heal as well.

Another couple shared that their son had been on drugs and they both realized that day that they were not helping him by sending him their thoughts of fear and hopelessness. Both of them had experienced the surge of heat and energy radiate from their hands. I responded by telling them that their son felt those same energies and that they should send the healing thoughts to him daily. They both excitedly said they would.

Lying in my hotel bed that evening I felt that everyone in the lecture room that day received what they needed, whether it was hope, a healing, or just hearing someone say "I love you." I thanked God and the angels for their help and, as I placed my hands over my heart with my thoughts repeating, "I am Light, Love, and Healing; I am Light, Love, and Healing," I drifted into a deep sleep.

It seemed like the true purpose of my life was unfolding before me. I was living more comfortably now having a nice home to live in with my new girlfriend, Amy. We fell in love in a French bakery where we learned that we shared the same values and vision of love and happiness for the world—I through my healing work, and she through a multimedia entertainment production company called RainbowLight Creations that brings uplifting messages of hope, love, and healing to humanity. Together, we made many new and loving friends who had also chosen to be in service to others. My needs were being met in all aspects of my life, and every day I was in gratitude. But we knew our life work was just beginning and that there was much to do.

While I traveled around to different states to honor lecturing requests and to teach as many people as possible the Mastery of Energy Healing technique, it always felt good to come home to Phoenix, Arizona. After completing a few months of traveling, I did the first of many monthly lectures nearby at Border's bookstore in Avondale. Twenty to thirty people attended my first lectures, and, as time passed, bookstore employees had to hustle at the last minute to find additional seating for the many people who came for healing and to learn more about energy healing.

I scheduled a free bookstore lecture to be held a few days before Christmas in 2006 that I called "A Free Gift of Holiday Healing." I saw it an opportunity to touch many more people, and to give everyone who wanted healing the opportunity by teaching them how to nurture themselves. I asked twenty or so of my students to assist me that evening. (I was always searching for healing opportunities for students, because practicing healing built up their healing skills and confidence.) Sitting in front of an audience with over 100 people that night, like I had done so many times before, I closed my eyes and meditated for a few minutes. After opening my eyes, I greeted the large gathering and told them I needed volunteers. More than fifty hands shot into the air!

I chose a young boy who was about six years old and a girl who was five after I was given permission from their parents that they could participate. I asked the two young children to join me at the front of the room. When both stood facing the group, I walked to a woman in a wheelchair who appeared to be in her late sixties and fighting tears. Extending my hand in a welcoming gesture, I placed my arms under her arms, around her back, and tightly hugged her. Assisted by her daughter and the person sitting next to her, the woman was gently escorted out of her wheelchair to my chair at the front of the room. The daughter informed the audience that her mother had fallen at home while dressing to attend that night's lecture. She was experiencing pain in her right shoulder, and there were a couple of noticeable black and blue bruises and swelling on her mother's arm. She added that even before the fall her mother regularly suffered from pain and had been physically challenged for the past several years due to fibromyalgia and rheumatoid arthritis.

I directed the young boy to stand at the woman's right side and the young girl to stand at her left, place their hands on the woman's shoulders, close their eyes, and send her love. While doing what was asked of them, I noticed an expression of pure concentration on the boy's face and a look of peace on the young girl's face. I looked around the room while everyone focused on the children. The room was so quiet you could have heard the sound of butterfly wings flapping. I walked toward two large bookshelves standing against a wall at the side of the room. I selected and scanned a book on European vacations for four or five minutes before placing it back on the shelf. Then I returned to the front of the room, knowing that no one would have noticed that I had left. I asked all three participants to open their eyes, and I directed the children to remove their hands from the woman. I asked the young girl if she felt anything while her eyes were closed and she excitedly said she felt bubbles coming out of her hands. I said, "Good for you!" Then I asked the boy if he felt anything, and he replied that he felt heat and power. I said, "That was good." I asked the children to return to their seats.

Next, I asked the woman if she could share her experience with us. She began to describe her sensations to the audience, which included a flow of energy. While describing the energy, she suddenly realized that her arms, including the swollen arm, were extended in the air above her head and she wasn't experiencing any pain. She excitedly yelled to the audience, "Look at my arm! Look at my arm!" Shock was written on her face and the faces in the audience as they witnessed these two small children with only an intent of pure love relieve her pain and reduce the woman's swelling by at least eighty percent. This all happened in less than five minutes! Now lightheaded, the woman stood and walked back to her chair without assistance.

I shared with the audience, "If we all possessed pure faith like these two young children, imagine what could be accomplished, not only for ourselves, but for the world."

After the lecture, people lined up to receive Light, Love, and Healing from my students and me. Meanwhile, customers continued to arrive at the bookstore to shop. Some shoppers took a place in line and waited for a healing after asking what was happening. A young woman holding her two-year-old son told me her son suffered from severe asthma, and doctors and medications weren't able to help him. Her son used a nebulizer machine several times a week to help him breathe. I looked into the young boy's eyes, placed my right hand on his chest, and with my thoughts said, "I send you Light, Love, and Healing, little one." A powerful energy of heat moved out through my hand. After a minute or so, as he smiled at me, I pulled my hand away from the child's chest. After handing her son to her boyfriend nearby, his mother asked if I could help her uncle who was in a hospital dying of cancer. I asked if she had a photograph of her uncle. She didn't, but she had a picture of him in her cell phone's memory. Quickly pulling the phone out of her purse, she opened it to show me his picture. I placed my hand about four inches from the phone and sent Light, Love, and Healing to her uncle. She quickly thanked me and stepped aside so the next person in line could receive a healing.

While placing my hand on the chest of the next person, I quickly glanced at my students. All of them were hard at work sending Light, Love, and Healing to people sitting on chairs lined up in front of them. More than three hours passed before we were done for the evening. Incredibly, they seemed fueled by the healing energies and the chance to help people in need. Some of them had even suffered from their own illnesses at one time, including Glen, and after they were healed they wanted to give to others. Their own healings inspired them to learn the Mastery of Energy Healing technique.

After everyone wanting a healing had left for home, I thanked my twenty students for being a part of that night with me, and I shared with them that many people were healed that night because of their love and compassion. Many of these students were first my clients and, after healing, became students. They wanted to learn how to take care of themselves and their loved ones, and then give hope and healing to others. Some of these students were new to energy healing, while others had been with me for years. A friend quickly took a picture of our group. We thanked each other, shared our goodnights and holiday blessings, and left for our homes. Without a doubt, that was the most beautiful Christmas event I had ever experienced.

Weeks after the bookstore Christmas event, a man in his mid-thirties came in for his scheduled appointment. He asked if I remembered him from the "Free Gift of Holiday Healing" event at the Avondale bookstore. "You sent healing to my girlfriend's severely asthmatic two-year-old son and to her uncle, who was in the hospital with cancer," he reminded me.

"Yes, I remember the little boy. How is he doing?"

"Her son woke the morning after the healing relieved from his asthma symptoms and he hasn't taken medication. Her uncle was released from the hospital two days after the healing event and is doing well."

I enthusiastically told him, "That's all wonderful news!"

I have done many similar events throughout Arizona and the United States, and I am always amazed yet humbled by the results and stories of healing from these events. My focus is to continue reaching out to bring the awareness to *everyone* that we *all have the gift to heal ourselves and others.* This is my heart's greatest desire.

# CHAPTER FIFTEEN

# A DAY OF GIVING

# Fall 2006

While talking with my girlfriend, Amy, who is also my office manager, one day during September 2006, I mentioned that I would like to help people in the Phoenix area struggling with cancer. "What do you suggest?" she asked.

Taking a few minutes before answering, I replied, "How about a 'free' day of healing for them?" She liked the idea. Soon after, a date was scheduled. The event was called "Free Healings for Individuals with Cancer." After we submitted a press release to the local news media, a television news reporter contacted my office requesting an interview with several of my clients and me. I suggested Glen, a client who had been healed of severe heart disease, and Christine, was previously bedridden for three years with severe migraines and healed of painful headaches in one healing session, for the interview.

The reporter was a very pleasant person, and I hoped that she understood energy healing to accurately report the facts. Several days later we received an e-mail saying that the interview would air on their station on September 20th. Unsure of how the reporter would ultimately present energy healing to her viewing audience or if viewers would accept the interview in a positive light, I made a promise to myself beforehand to continue doing healing work and help people regardless of the outcome.

The televised report mentioned two people in despair because they suffered from severe illnesses that the traditional medical community was unable to help. Still, there was hope for people like them. Glen and Christine told their stories about being healed of their ailments.

Later that evening, I received multiple calls from viewers who saw the report, and the following day more than three hundred people called from all around Arizona. The calls continued for weeks, and during the following six months I encountered countless types of physical and emotional illness that people had to deal with. I also witnessed miracles of spontaneous healings of many of those illnesses. Some clients shared with me that they had experienced out-of-body episodes and journeys into the Light during their illnesses or surgeries, and I happily shared my own experience with them. Others said they saw or felt angels, Jesus, Mother Mary, Buddha, and other heavenly beings.

During these hectic months Amy, her assistant, and I worked very long days. Clients shared with us that we were their last hope, so we were determined to make ourselves available to them, whatever it took on our part to do that.

At one point during this busy time, a client named Diane returned for her second appointment. Her son patiently sat in the waiting room while Diane and I talked in my office.

"Diane, it's been six weeks since your first appointment for the tumor in your head. I'm curious: Have the doctors found any change?" I asked.

"Alex, the tumor was the size of a golf ball when I last saw you. Two days after my visit with you an MRI was done and it showed the tumor had shrunk by fifty-five percent! The nurse cried when she saw the results," Diane reported.

"That's great! I'm so happy for you," I said.

Following her second healing session, I suggested to Diane I would like her to return for another appointment. She looked at me and, with a smile on her face, she said, "Alex, I know the tumor is gone now.

Thank you." She made it clear that, in her opinion, additional visits would be unnecessary.

"Diane, if we never see each other again, it's been my pleasure knowing you."

"Thank you for your help, Alex."

Sometimes during healing sessions I observed orbs of flashing lights right next to my clients. One day Linda came to my office to discover more about her spirituality, not because of an illness. An attractive lady in her late forties, she cared deeply about her family. With her lying on the table with her eyes closed, I placed my hands over her body. Closing my eyes, I saw flashes of white light and felt energy begin to flow from my hands. Linda's face was glowing as she opened her eyes, and I asked about her experience. She seemed dazed, like she was someplace else, and it took her a while to answer me.

"Alex, when I closed my eyes I began to see lights flashing all around and the lights turned into angels with beautiful wings. A being appeared with the angels, and it was Jesus."

"Linda, now you know who is always with you," I replied.

Wishing her well, I walked her out of the office and returned to prepare for my next client. Placing my hands on my chest to bring in Light, Love, and Healing, I thanked God for allowing me to be part of His love for us.

I never worked so hard, physically and especially emotionally, in my entire life. I wondered how long I could keep up the frenetic pace. It was hard for me to slow down because I got energized, for instance, when someone in a wheelchair was brought to see me after steadfastly enduring pain for years and then, after the healing session, was able to walk out of my office under his or her own power. During that time and to the present day, I often experience an overwhelming sense of reverence and humility in my heart for the work I am privileged to do.

I'm so grateful for the special gift God has given me and for my eventual acceptance to use His gift to help others. I know my mother and father are very happy with the work I am doing, even though they didn't understand it while they were alive. Now that they are in Heaven they understand perfectly, and they often appear in my office smiling and holding hands while I do healing work.

After the news report aired on television, it was more than six months before my life returned to a normal pace. It may sound astonishing, but we do not recall any negative feedback from the public or otherwise after this report aired. Though not every client received what they wanted, I believe they received what they needed: hope, a healing, or a miracle.

The press release Amy prepared on the free cancer-healing event at the office in September was sent to a number of news programs. One person stepped forward to investigate and report on the event. I wonder to this day if that reporter could ever comprehend the number of lives and families she helped in only four minutes one late evening in September 2006.

# CHAPTER SIXTEEN

# AN ANGEL
# OF HEALING

## Winter 2006

My first client of the day was Judy, and I was looking forward to meeting and helping her. It was December 2006, and ten years already passed since my life-changing visit to San Luis, Mexico.

Judy lived in northern Arizona, a two-hour drive each way to my Phoenix office. A single mother in her sixties, Judy adopted three children who were then teenagers. I invited Judy into my healing room and offered her a seat next to my desk. I couldn't help notice how the left side of her face was drawn downward. I assumed her facial condition was the result of a stroke.

Sitting in the chair, she first just stared at me for what seemed like forever and then began to describe an experience she had late one night. Judy said she was sound asleep in her bed when she was awakened by the fragrance of roses. The aroma grew stronger and stronger, and when she opened her eyes she saw that her entire bedroom was filled with a white mist, like the cloudy mist in a garden. She said everything was vivid and unforgettable, and she felt incredibly peaceful. Near the foot of her bed on the wall she could see a dimly glowing light with a halo around it. She said she stared at it for a moment trying to figure out what was happening and where she was. She then heard a soft voice say, "You are going to be okay." Judy told me she was thinking she must be crazy because she was hearing a voice coming out of the wall. Again, the voice said, "You are going to be okay," and then the light faded away.

Judy continued, telling me she wasn't afraid of the voice. She later realized the voice was telling her she was not alone. She felt that this incredible experience was a sign that change would happen, providing a better future for her. I asked if the voice she heard was one she recognized. She replied simply, "It was God." Judy said that several days after that experience she happened to see a dramatic television news story featuring a man who had suffered from heart disease and me. The man on the show had seen some of the most renowned cardiologists in the country and undergone a number of experimental stem cell procedures within a year's time, with no positive outcome. His doctors told him he had only one to two years to live, and he often seriously contemplated suicide. Judy remembered from the news story that the man's doctor confirmed, after seeing me for healing treatments, that he no longer had heart disease. Judy said to me, "Alex, when I saw you on television, I just knew that God wanted me to see you."

Judy described her multiple ailments. Because she suffered a stroke a month before, she had no feeling on the left side of her face; it was numb. She had severe headaches and poor circulation in both of her legs. Judy also experienced constant pain in her left heel, right knee, and lower back from three bad discs, and her hip needed surgical replacement.

While relaxing music played in the background, I invited Judy to lie down on the healing table, and she closed her eyes. I didn't know what to expect for Judy, but I hoped she would be healed of her ailments. I placed my hands above her body and suddenly a burst of brilliant white light startled me and illuminated the small room. I knew the angels were there with us. With my eyes now closed, the healing energies began to flow through my body. I saw waves of color, one following the other: white light, then gold, then green, then blue. It felt like it was 100 degrees in the room but I knew the thermostat was secured at seventy-two. After approximately forty minutes I gently touched Judy's left hand and woke her from a restful state. When she opened her eyes she had a big, beautiful smile on her face.

She took a couple of moments before saying, "This was one of the most incredible experiences." As she said this, she brought both of her hands up to touch her face. She touched her cheeks and her forehead, moved her opened fingers to her temples, and exclaimed, "*I am healed!*" Her eyes now opened wide, she continued excitedly, "I'm healed of my stroke, Alex!" She couldn't help feeling her face as in disbelief.

She eagerly told me that, during her session, she heard a voice next to her on the right side of her head. It said, "Do not be afraid. You will be okay." Then, she said she felt the wings of an angel caressing the left side of her face. She continued, "I thought, 'How could this be? I have a stroke. I'm not supposed to feel anything.' Then this bright luminous light began to shine in my face, and I felt this warmth. It began to spread out through my entire body. Then, I heard you call my name, 'Judy. Your time is up.' I am healed, Alex. My face is healed!"

After listening to Judy tell her story, I finally got a chance to hug her. I said, "That's an incredible experience you had, and I'm blessed and grateful to have been a part of it, but you healed yourself, my friend. The angel and I were just here to assist."

Before leaving, Judy gave me another big hug. I closed the door and walked across the room to my desk feeling great joy from the healing that just occurred. I felt that it was Judy's faith in God that allowed healing to take place. When one has faith, miraculous things happen.

My thoughts wandered for a moment as I pondered all the experiences that I had gone through over the previous ten years. I didn't know it at the time, but I was gaining the wisdom I needed to understand myself more deeply so I could be the man that I truly am: a man of Light, Love, and Healing. I learned that everything I needed to create

"Heaven on Earth" was already within me; I only needed to tap into the higher energies of humility, gratitude, compassion, forgiveness, and love to experience great peace and joy. And I realized that by continuing to bring in Light, Love, and Healing energies to myself, I not only become it, but I can share it with others so we *all* may bring to us our heart's desires.

But I had no time to ponder. Sitting down on my chair at my desk, I began to prepare for my next client. Placing my hands on my chest I whispered softly to myself, "*I am Light, Love, and Healing. I am Light, Love, and Healing.*"

# A FINAL WORD

*"Humility, compassion, and love*
*are the foundations of wisdom,*
*and with that wisdom*
*one can heal himself and assist others in healing,*
*raising the consciousness of humanity."*

—Alex J. Hermosillo

# APPENDIX A

# MASTERY OF ENERGY HEALING

## Healing Exercises

**Healing Yourself**

Your body and consciousness have stored a complete record of every experience in your life since the moment you were born. Some experiences have nurtured your light body energies, and some have depleted your light body energies. When enough negative life experiences have accumulated, especially if you hold on to them consciously or unconsciously, your light body energy dims and you are no longer able to function efficiently emotionally, mentally, physically, and even spiritually.

To offer a metaphor, imagine your light body as a giant computer that is infected with harmful viruses. The results of these harmful viruses include emotions such as stress, fear, worry, grief, guilt, shame, anger, and judgment toward yourself and others, as well as physical diseases such as arthritis, diabetes, high blood pressure, heart disease, and cancer, to name a few. All you need to do is delete the negative information or harmful viruses from the computer. Here is an exercise to release these negative non-nurturing energies so your light body may be strong and shine brightly.

Please keep in mind that these exercises are to be utilized as a *support* to healing emotionally, mentally, physically, and spiritually in combination with professional medical care.

## Step 1—Release Negative Energies

In a quiet place, sit down with your hands on your lap or, if more comfortable, lie down with your arms at your side. With your thoughts, say to yourself,

> *"I now release from every cell of my body,*
> *from my heart, and from my mind*
> *confusion."*

Take a deep breath of white light. Visualize and *feel* it dissipating all negativity of confusion from your body and mind. Exhale.

Next, with your thoughts, say to yourself,

> *"I now release from every cell of my body,*
> *from my heart, and from my mind*
> doubt."

Take a deep breath of white light. Visualize and *feel* it dissipating all negativity of doubt from your body and mind. Exhale.

Next, with your thoughts, say to yourself,

> *"I now release from every cell of my body,*
> *from my heart, and from my mind*
> stress."

Take a deep breath of white light. Visualize and *feel* it dissipating all negativity of stress from your body and mind. Exhale.

Next, with your thoughts, say to yourself,

> *"I now release from every cell of my body,*
> *from my heart, and from my mind*
> fear."

Take a deep breath of white light. Visualize and *feel* it dissipating all negativity of fear from your body and mind. Exhale.

Next, with your thoughts, say to yourself,

> *"I now release from every cell of my body,*
> *from my heart, and from my mind*
> _____."

In the blank space, say the name of any emotional attribute or physical disease that you want to release. (Examples include shame, guilt, worries, anger, judgment, heartache, heartbreak, grief, hatred, unworthiness, being a victim, toxins and poisons from drugs or alcohol, arthritis, headaches, backaches, depression, tumors, etc.) You can even release traumatizing people and events that you experienced in your life. Fill in the blank with experiences such as the grief from the separation of a loved one due to his or her transition or possibly a breakup of a relationship (romantic or family), or even with an animal companion. Other examples include emotional or physical abuse experiences from parents, relatives, or friends, or even an argument you had with a co-worker. You can release any negative emotion, physical disease, traumatizing person, and/or event that has caused you pain.

Take a deep breath of white light and state what you want to release. Visualize the white light dissipating all negativity from your body and mind. Exhale as you *feel* this negative energy leaving the top of your head flowing downward through your body and out of your hands and feet.

You could even say,

> *"I now release all energies and all life experiences that created my emotional distress and physical disease."*

You are releasing the accumulation of negative energies from your life experiences or, using the metaphor of the computer, deleting the virus programs that you no longer want.

## Step 2—Bring in Positive Healing Energies

Now that you have released the negative energies, you are going to fill that empty space with positive nurturing and healing energies or, still using the metaphor of the computer, install new programs.

Continue your healing exercise by placing both of your hands, one overlapping the other, on the center of your chest. With your thoughts, say to yourself,

*"I now bring into every cell of my body, into my heart, and into my mind*
Light, Love, and Healing!"

Take a deep breath, filling your heart, lungs, spine, nervous system, and every cell of your body with the energy of Light, Love, and Healing. Visualize that light as brilliant white. Imagine in your mind's eye that even your hands are now pure white light heating up, dissipating any residual negativity, and charging up your light body energy. Repeat three times in a row, or until you feel yourself become lighter, brighter, peaceful, calm, and relaxed.

### Step 3—Bring in Healing Energies to a Specific Body Area

Next, if you have a specific area of your body that is painful or needs special attention (torn ligament in your knee, broken arm, cancer of the stomach, tumors in the breast area, heart disease in the heart area, or forehead for headaches), you can focus sending healing energies to that area. Place your hand or hands on the problem area and, with your thoughts, say to yourself,

*"I now bring into my [name area of body]*
*Light, Love, and Healing!"*

Take a deep breath of pure white light, visualizing your hands turning brilliant white. Send that white light energy through your hands to the problem area turning that area bright light also. *Feel* that light dissipate any remaining negative energies that created the pain or disease, bringing an unbalanced energy area to balance and perfect health.

Repeat bringing in healing energies to a specific body area three times per day.

As mentioned earlier in the book, sensations you may experience during these exercises include the heating up of the hand(s), coolness of the hand(s), tingling sensations, a magnetic pull, and a sensation of energy flowing out of the hand(s) and into the body, which might be described as an energetic flow of water. Others include a prickly or needle sensation of the hand(s). All of these sensations are common. Some of you will feel these sensations the first time, while others may need to practice to become more aware and sensitive to the different energies. Know that with your intent the healing energies *are* flowing and you are reprogramming the cells of your body to be Light, Love, and Healing. Where there is intent, energy flows. It is a universal law of Creation.

Depending on what you're working through emotionally, mentally, physically, and even spiritually, for best results it is recommended that one does this entire exercise for thirty days in a row, three times per day (morning, afternoon, and evening). After thirty days, a decision can be made whether to continue as before, or taper off by doing the exercises twice a day, or even once daily. I now do this process twice a day: first thing in the morning before I start my day, and in the evening before going to bed.

The more you practice bringing in Light, Love, and Healing into yourself, the more you will *become* Light, Love, and Healing, and you will begin to see and experience positive changes in your life.

For those of you on the spiritual path, bringing in Light, Love, and Healing daily will raise your consciousness to a higher vibration walking the steps toward enlightenment, for we are beings of light, love is what created us, and healing energies sustains us on Earth.

*For those of you who wish to have additional assistance, I have created a simple but powerful guided meditation in CD format. Information about how to order can be found at www.masteryofenergyhealing.com.*

## ASSISTING OTHERS WITH HEALING

It's important to state here that before you can assist another in healing, you must first be and emanate the energies of Light, Love, and Healing. Consider yourself a battery charger from your local auto parts store that is not functioning properly. How can you, the charger, give energy to charge up someone else's battery if you are lacking the energy and power to provide for him or her? The first step in this exercise will assist you in charging yourself up to ensure that you will have the energy and power to assist others.

### Step I—Charge Your Light Energy Body

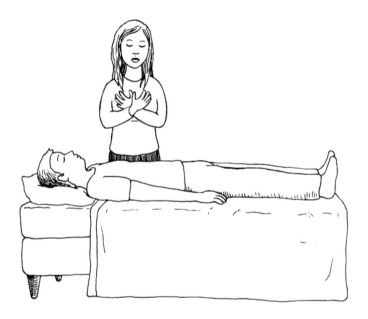

Place both of your hands, one overlapping the other, on the center of your chest. Take a deep breath, visualizing your breath as bright white light filling up your heart, your chest, and every cell of your body as you begin to see your hands glow with white light. With your thoughts, say to yourself,

> *"I now bring into every cell of my body, my heart, and mind*
> Light, Love, and Healing!"

*Feel* these powerful healing energies building and expanding throughout your body. Exhale and repeat this step two more times, or until you can feel you are radiating brilliant white light. Imagine yourself as the sun with an infinite supply of light.

## Step 2—Send Healing Energies

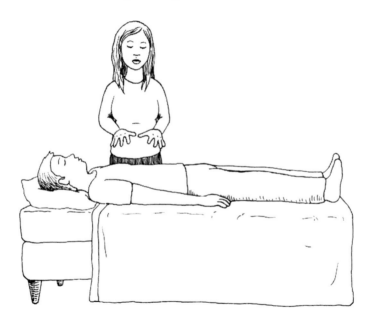

Place both of your hands one to four inches above the person's body where his or her pain or illness is located. You can say either out loud or with your thoughts,

*"We now send to you,*
Light, Love, and Healing!"

Visualize that your hands are glowing with brilliant white light as the love and healing energies are sent to the person dissipating all energies that created the illness. Do this for ten minutes, three times per day if time permits. Remember that intent overrides technique, and your intent is Light, Love, and Healing.

If you feel so inclined, it's okay to ask for help. That's why I say, "We now send to you...." I see the angels, and they are with us all. They are always happy to assist!

Keep in mind when you are assisting another with healing that you do not absorb their pain. We always want to be the Light for him or her. To sustain the energies of Light, Love, and Healing for yourself and others, practice your exercises daily.

The Light contains all wisdom of creation, including the wisdom of nurturing and healing. This is the simplicity of it. Do not worry that you are doing these exercise incorrectly, and do not be attached to the outcome. Healing happens on many different levels (emotional, mental, physical, and spiritual) and in its own time. People's healing is between them and God. Your job is to simply be Light, Love, and Healing to assist the healing process. We call this "let go and let God."

# APPENDIX B

# MASTERY OF ENERGY HEALING CLASSES

I offer the Mastery of Energy Healing (M.E.H.) technique to the public. Everyone is born with the gift of healing, and I am here to remind you of the inherent gifts you hold.

I thank God for the gift of healing that was awakened within me, along with all of my life learning experiences, and I am committed to lecturing and teaching as many people as possible this simple yet powerful technique, which utilizes sources that are readily available to all of us, called Light, Love, and Healing.

I wrote this book because I want people to know that they can place their hands on themselves and simply say, "I now bring in Light, Love, and Healing," and begin to nurture their thoughts, emotions, physical body, and spirit. Further, I want people to know that if they have a loved one at home or in a hospital, they can place their hands on him or her, and simply with their thoughts send Light, Love, and Healing to comfort and nurture that person.

M.E.H. is a gentle, non-invasive process that is simple, fast, and effective. Anyone can learn this technique in a one-day class to assist themselves and others, in person or at a distance. Students and clients come from all walks of life, including artists, teachers, homemakers, nurses, doctors, athletes, and anyone interested in nurturing himself or herself so they may live their fullest potential.

Many of my clients take the classes and have healed themselves, only to turn around and utilize the technique to assist others in healing. The message that I give to my clients and students is that we are here to have a happy, healthy, and loving life. That is my wish for them, and that is my wish for you!

In service,

Alex J. Hermosillo

Visit www.masteryofenergyhealing.com for more info on upcoming lectures and classes.

# GLOSSARY

This glossary was created to assist readers who are new to some of the terms in this book. Use it as a source of reference, understanding that everyone has their own truth based on their life experiences. The definitions in this glossary are based on the experiences in my life.

**Angel:** messengers of God providing humanity with wisdom, peace, inspiration, healing, and love.

**Aura:** the energies that emanate and encircle the physical body and that are produced due to one's life experiences including their thoughts, emotions, actions, and beliefs

**Balanced energies:** energies that were once unbalanced creating disharmony in the physical, emotional, mental, and spirit bodies, and that have been balanced creating harmony

**Buddha:** Siddhartha Gautama was a spiritual teacher from ancient India who founded Buddhism; he was regarded as "The Buddha," meaning "enlightened one"

**Consciousness:** the amount of Light a person holds in their body, mind, and spirit; the Light holds information and wisdom of the universe and God

**Dense energies:** an accumulation of negativity creating distress in the body, mind, and spirit

**Emotional pain:** negative and hurtful events of the past that are stored in the cells of the body that produce thoughts and emotions of grief, fear, depression, and stress to name a few, all which deplete one's physical body and their Light

**Empathic:** the ability to emotionally and physically feel and/or sense what another person is experiencing

**Energy:** the substance of all creation in the physical and non-physical; the material that makes up the flesh and spirit

**Energy vibration:** all creation contains energy vibrations of different frequencies and rates; in the physical world the energy vibration of a flower vibrates higher than a rock; in the non-physical world the emotion of love vibrates much higher than fear

**Ethereal bodies:** the energy of light produced by angels; the spirit of those who have transitioned to Heaven; the 4th dimension; the 'other side'

**Expanded Awareness:** the realization that one did not have before, bringing a wider, and oftentimes, higher and more objective perception about people, events, circumstances, and their own life as a whole

**Flesh body:** our physical body

**God:** creator of all, the most powerful and infinite divine energy of Light; the all loving, all knowing; Great Spirit

**Healing:** bringing back to wholeness or harmony a person's spiritual, emotional, mental, and physical bodies

**Healing Energies:** the energy that nurtures a person's body, mind, and spirit

**Heaven:** where one's soul (spirit energy body) goes to after life on earth; a place of pure peace, love, and joy being one with God

**Heaven on Earth:** when one releases fear, shame, grief, anger, judgment towards themselves and others for example, their thoughts, emotions, and expression of self shifts to gratitude, peace, joy, compassion, humility, forgiveness, and love for themselves, others, and the world

**Heavenly beings:** angels, Jesus, Buddha, Mother Mary, and other beings that reside in Heaven who bring guidance, protection, support, and healing to mankind

**Higher Consciousness:** consciousness is the amount of information one has; the higher consciousness of a person, the more pure information they have of themselves, others, the universe, and God; the highest state of consciousness is often described as enlightenment

**Jesus:** Jesus of Nazareth, known as the Messiah, the anointed one, Christ; performed miracle healings through humility, compassion, and love

**Light:** the essence of our soul; the spark of life; and the material that makes up our mind, body, spirit, and soul

**Light, Love, and Healing:** positive energies that nurture, bring healing, and support the mind, body, and spirit; bringing in these energies daily will assist in raising one's consciousness

**Mastery of Energy Healing:** a simple technique created by Alex to assist in releasing unserving energies of emotions, thought patterns, and physical illness such as fear, worries, grief, and cancer that do not nurture the mind, body, and spirit, and then bringing in positive energies such as gratitude, peace, joy, and love that do nurture and bring healing to the mind, body, and spirit; also the name of Alex's company

**Meditation:** a state of deep relaxation, to be in a state of peace, to go within oneself and practice being in the 'now'

**Mother Mary:** the mother of Jesus of Nazareth, also known as the Virgin Mary

**Near-death experience:** when the spirit of the physical body leaves the body for a limited time, then returns

**Negative energies:** thoughts, words, and actions such as shame, guilt, anger, fear, and judgment towards yourself and others that do not nurture one's mind, body, and spirit creating emotional distress, physical illness, and spiritual disharmony, preventing one from living their fullest potential

**Non-physical world:** the world beyond physical form and matter; the 4th dimension and beyond; metaphysical; examples include thoughts, emotions, light, sound, angels, and other heavenly beings

**Orb:** transparent balls of light holding the energy of heavenly beings; sometimes appear translucent which can be seen with the naked eyes or when captured in digital photos and videos

**Out-of-body experience:** a floating sensation outside of one's own body, leaving the physical body and perceiving it from another place

**Physical pain:** suffering or distress of the body

**Physical world:** that which is material and matter; of the body as opposed to the mind; the three-dimensional world filled with objects; examples include food, trees, animals, water, the body, planets, and stars

**Psychic senses:** the ability to know and gain information through one's intuition, or 6th sense, about a person, object or event past, present, and future

**Reiki:** developed by Buddhist, Mikao Usui in 1922, transferring life force healing energy from the palms of a practitioner to assist in healing

**Sign:** a message of guidance you recognize for yourself that can come in many ways, providing meaningful insight or a deeper understanding, and bringing one feelings of support, peace, and joy; examples include - lyrics in a song, a passage in a book, a conversation, a dream, or repetitive thoughts

**Spirit [body]:** is the energy created by and connected to your soul

**Spontaneous healing:** a complete cure of unexpected improvement of disease, physical, mental, and/or emotional

**Unbalanced energies:** when the human body is in disharmony, out of balance creating emotional distress and/or physical disease

**Vibrational being:** we are beings of light, and the light holds information including every experience a person has which is stored in the cells of their body—our positive experiences as well as our negative ones—and the body vibrates this energy and information

# HEALING TESTIMONIALS

*Read about 'real-life' healing experiences from clients and students of Mastery of Energy Healing. These stories are shared by the individuals below to give others hope, healing, and even miracles.*

"My eighteen-month old son, Leo, had been diagnosed with a testicular tumor, and his blood tests revealed markers for cancer. The specialist said this type of cancer spreads quickly, so we had to do immediate surgery to remove the testicle. We called Alex Hermosillo who graciously agreed to do a long distant healing on Leo. Leo came through the surgery with flying colors and was able to come home immediately afterward. Days later, we received the astounding results from the lab that there had been absolutely no cancer cells present in the testicular tumor. The oncologist, not believing the results, had the sample sent to a special lab conference for difficult to diagnose tumors. Again, the results came back with no dead or alive cancer cells present. I believe that miracle was the healing performed by Alex Hermosillo, and I am eternally grateful. To this day, Leo is cancer and tumor free with no need for any chemotherapy or radiation treatments."
    *Patricia B.*

"After seeing Alex, I went from being confined to a scooter, on oxygen, and taking up to thirty-two pills in the morning for my heart condition, to ballroom dancing, walking two to three miles at a time and only one pill for my diabetes. I was taking up to sixteen nitroglycerin pills per day to keep the pain down, but have not used any in eight months. I am back to my active self. Alex is not only a healer, but also a good friend and teacher."

Glen P.

"After years of severe Post Partum Depression being medicated with prescription drugs and supplements, I sought the help of Alex J. Hermosillo. After only one healing session with him, I couldn't believe how much better I felt. I had immediate relief of 80% from my depression. It's been a year and a half, and I'm depression-free! Thanks Alex for helping me get my life back, not just for me, but also for my children who need their mom to be healthy. I am FOREVER grateful!"

Lilia A.

"Having been diagnosed with a large Teratoma (tumor) on my right ovary, and surgery scheduled for its removal, Alex sent me healing energies for a completely different health issue I was dealing with. Even without knowledge of the tumor, and following a sharp pain, which I felt during the session in that area of my body, Alex said to me, "The angels say they allowed you to feel the pain, so you would know it was gone." Following an exam and ultrasound with my regular physician, the tests revealed a completely normal ovary! My doctor was dumfounded. I decided to take Alex's MEH classes to learn how to perform energy healing on myself and loved ones, which I have found very helpful! Thank you, Alex, for sharing your love, wisdom, and light!"

Joy C.

"In 2007, I was diagnosed with Breast Cancer. I had surgery, chemo, and was on the road to recovery. In February 2008, I went to the dentist because my mouth would not heal after the chemo. He sent me to an implant specialist who took X rays and said the bone in my upper jaw was shrinking causing the implants to loosen. When I returned home, my sister told me about Alex, and I made the call to his office. After one private session with him, all mouth sores were gone, and the implants were tight. I went back to the specialist, and after his second exam said, 'If I hadn't taken the X rays myself I wouldn't believe that you are the same person who came to me two weeks ago. Whatever you did, keep it up, you don't need me.'

Then, in October 2008, I went for my yearly check up. My surgeon, who is the chief of staff at the Breast Center at my local hospital, ordered a mammogram. The results were a tumor on the right breast. They also saw a lot of scar tissue from the reconstruction surgery that had occurred after the first round of breast cancer in 2007. I saw Alex for a healing, then returned to my surgeon where he examined me. He couldn't find the tumor, so he ordered an ultrasound and MRI. The results were that the tumor and the scar tissue were gone. My doctor. wished me well with instructions for a follow up visit next year. Alex is not only my dear friend, but also my teacher, and he and his office staff have become very dear friends."

*Adele F.*

"Alex Hermosillo's energy healing has totally and completely transformed my life. I experienced a difficult childhood and a stressful marriage of 27 years. After attending his first class, my life was forever changed. I not only was healed of all my past negative energies and emotions, but I also found that I was blessed to be able to perform energy healings on my surgical patients as well. As an OR nurse, there is no greater joy than to see patients receive spontaneous healings intraoperatively. I now live my life happy, healthy, and in control. I feel such gratitude to Alex for allowing me to experience energy healing and the peace, joy, and love that comes as a result of negative energy release."

*Jeanne D.*

"My father was diagnosed with blockages in his heart and was scheduled for surgery the next morning. I called Alex Hermosillo, and after sending him a photo of dad, Alex sent healing energies long distance. The next morning, the doctors discovered, mysteriously, the blockages had disappeared. Everyone agreed it was nothing short of a miracle! Thank you, Alex, God, and the angels for healing my dad!"

*Randy B.*

"I have had the good fortune of meeting Alex at one of his lectures. His spirit is that of love and peace, and he presents teachings that all can learn from. His guidance to a deeper understanding of our spiritual journey is truly one of the many blessings that he offers. My experience with Alex's *Mastery of Energy Healing* has left me with a greater awareness of how to release the lower frequencies I have held inside."

*R. V.*

"Alex has extraordinary skills. I had chronic sinus headaches in the past, and after working with Alex, now they are rare. I require less sleep and have much more energy. I see the world differently, and I appreciate the beauty of everyday things. 'Everything is perfect.' Alex is also the most inspirational teacher I have ever had. I have learned so much from him in such a short time!"

*Julie G.*

"I had been dealing with chronic pain in my feet for over five years. I tried everything the doctors suggested, but I still found it a struggle to walk most of the time, especially at night. I attended one of Alex's lectures and received a strong gift of healing. The pain in my feet was healed 100%, and today my energy is far better too. Thank you, Alex."

*Michael M.*

"I have used the "*I NOW RELEASE, I NOW BRING IN*" guided meditation CD since December 14, 2006. I use it once per day, and I just want to say that this is an incredible tool to release the old sludge and garbage that fills our lives and stops us from spiritual evolution. I highly recommend this CD as a fantastic tool for healing old wounds and moving on to joy and peace in our lives."

*Michele M.*

"Dear Alex, thank you for making a difference in my life. I feel very lucky to have found you in the Achieve Radio archives. My heart has been deeply touched and opened with such softness by your powerful loving energy. It's just beautiful, and I want to thank you for creating your incredibly powerful, "I Now Release, I Now Bring In" CD. To me, it's the best thing I ever bought for myself. I almost can't believe that I'm able now to totally cleanse my whole being, and then fill up to the brim with love, power, beauty and joy, every day and at any time. It's so easy, very joyful, and really powerful. And wow...the heart-power of that music is something else! I know that all of this is bringing me into a much happier and more loving way of being in the world with myself and with others. I also have a sister who has become open to using your CD, and she too is bowled over by the incredibly loving healing power it holds and opens up in us. Thank you forever."

*Brigit E.*

# ABOUT THE AUTHOR

Alex J. Hermosillo is an internationally known spiritual teacher who was born with the gift of healing. As a young man, he had the ability to help people with their pain with a touch of his hand. In 1997, he journeyed to Heaven through a near-death experience where he gained great wisdom. He brings messages from Heaven and has helped people heal from heart disease, cancer, tumors, migraine headaches, grief, depression, and much more. With the gifts given to Alex, he developed a quick, simple, and effective energy healing method that anyone can do for themselves and others called, Mastery of Energy Healing. Alex dedicates his life to help others experience a peaceful, happy, and healthy life, what he calls, "Living Heaven on Earth."

Alex touches the lives of thousands who seek healing through his lectures, classes, and internet radio show, "The Happy Healer." He offers his services from his hometown in Phoenix, Arizona, as well as travels speaking and teaching at medical colleges, bookstores, related associations, and churches including I.A.N.D.S. (International Association for Near Death Studies), LECOM (Lake Erie College of Osteopathic Medicine), Southwest College of Naturopathic Medicine, and more. He has been featured on FOX 10 News (Phoenix, Arizona) and is published in various media.

To learn more about Alex J. Hermosillo, classes, and healing stories, go to www.masteryofenergyhealingcom.

CPSIA information can be obtained at www.ICGtesting.com
Printed in the USA
LVOW06s1126110814

398511LV00004B/6/P